The Search for Visible Unity

Baptism ◊ Eucharist ◊ Ministry

Jeffrey Gros
Editor

The Pilgrim Press
NEW YORK

Library of Congress Cataloging in Publication Data
Main entry under title:

The Search for visible unity.

   Papers and discussions from the Chicago Conference
on BEM Reception, Oct, 12-14, 1983.
   Includes bibliographical references.
   1. Baptism and Christian union—Congresses.
2. Lord's Supper and Christian union—Congresses.
3. Pastoral theology and Christian union—Congresses.
I. Gros, Jeffrey, 1938-
II. Chicago Conference on BEM Reception (1983)
BX9.5.S2S43   1984   234'.16   84-12112
ISBN 0-8298-0722-5 (pbk.)

The Pilgrim Press, 132 West 31 Street, New York, NY 10001

CONTENTS

BAPTISM, EUCHARIST, AND MINISTRY: INTRODUCTION

Jeffrey Gros

With the unanimous adoption of the *Baptism, Eucharist, and Ministry* (hereafter, BEM) statement by the Commission on Faith and Order of the World Council of Churches in Lima, Peru, in January, 1982, and the decision that it was mature enough to send to the churches, the worldwide movement toward reconciliation of the Christian churches has reached a new level of convergence. The Sixth Assembly of the World Council of Churches, meeting in Vancouver in the summer of 1983, reaffirmed the decision to send BEM to the churches for reception, asking for an initial response by December, 1984, and a more serious response by December, 1985, pointing the way toward a world conference on Faith and Order in 1987 or 1988. The production of the BEM text culminates fifty years of intense dialogue within the worldwide Faith and Order movement, contributed to by bilateral conversations, church unions effected on the basis of theological consensus, and decades of life and work together in the conciliar movement.

The W.C.C. places this text into the hands of the over 300 member churches —as well as those churches which are members of the Commission on Faith and Order, such as the Roman Catholic—for "reception." For the first time in history a text produced by such a diverse group of theologians on behalf of their churches is to be evaluated for action in the churches of a divided Christianity. Not only do many churches have no experience of "reception" of an ecumenical document, but there is also no clear and common agreement as to what "reception" would mean.

From October 12 to 14, 1983, at Hyde Park in Chicago, a conference was held bringing together more than twenty churches with the Commission on Faith and Order of the National Council of Churches and the theologians of the Hyde Park Cluster of Theological Schools to discuss the reception process in the

Jeffrey Gros (Roman Catholic), F.S.C., has been director of the Commission on Faith and Order of the National Council of Churches of Christ in the U.S.A. since January, 1983, prior to which he was Associate Director from 1981. He has a B.A. and an M.Ed. in biology education from St. Mary's College, Winona, MN; an M.A. in theology from Marquette University, Milwaukee, WI; and a Ph.D. (1973) in theology from Fordham University. He has done further study at Northwestern University, the University of Chicago, St. Louis University, Union Theological Seminary (N.Y.C.), the New School for Social Research, and the Hebrew Union College in Jerusalem. Brother Jeffrey taught for several years at the high school, adult ministry training, college, and seminary levels, as well as serving on diocesan ecumenical commissions and on the board of the National Association of Diocesan Ecumenical Officers. His articles and reviews have appeared in a wide variety of journals including *Christianity and Crisis*, *Dialog*, *The Ecumenical Review*, *Ecumenical Trends*, *Emmanuel*, *J.E.S.*, *Living Light*, *Mid-stream*, *Spiritual Life*, *Theological Studies*, and *Worship*. He has also delivered papers for several academic and professional organizations.

United States churches. The conference was generated and sponsored by the Ecumenical Project at Jesuit House, funded by the Lilly Foundation, and staffed at the local level by David Bowman, S.J. Over 150 theologians, church leaders, pastors, and involved ecumenists gathered from all over the United States and Canada to listen to serious theological reflection, to share the process of reception to be used in their own communions, and to plan together the ecumenical future of the reception process in the U.S. context.

The aims of the conference were manifold: communication among the churches as the process moves forward, the enrichment of each individual communion through sharing the experience of others, theological reflection on the nature of "reception," situating the reception of BEM within the context of the wider ecumenical movement, enriching the theological reflection of the Commission on Faith and Order of the National Council of Churches in its deliberations, providing services of theological reflection from the Hyde Park Cluster of Theological Schools to the churches and the Commission on Faith and Order, and providing a record of the "reception" processes and their contexts for the wider theological and church community through the publication of the papers and discussion. The purpose of this collection, therefore, is to provide resources for the church community, the scholarly community, and professional ecumenists.

The question of "reception" has been discussed extensively in the ecumenical theological community for some time. However, as the BEM document comes before the churches and as several of the bilateral conversations begin to reach maturity, we are at a stage in which the churches themselves and the seminary and graduate theological community are called to be more intimately involved. This requires a more precise and at the same time more accessible definition of what is meant by "reception." In the context of parliamentary procedure as understood in the West, reception tends to have a low-level sense of ownership.

However, seen in the historical context of the reception of the New Testament canon by the church and the deliberations and reception of the ancient creeds in the Councils of Nicaea (325), Constantinople (381), and Chalcedon (451), the theological and historical dimensions of reception take on a normative significance for many of the communions represented in the worldwide Faith and Order movement. In the period after the Reformation there were such events as the development of the Formula of Concord and its reception (1577), the reception of the decrees of the First and Second Vatican Councils in Roman Catholicism, and the reception of both the Confession of 1967 in the former United Presbyterian Church and the study of the Declaration of Faith in the 1970's by the former Presbyterian Church, U.S. While these processes have different characteristics, they can all illuminate the challenge laid before the churches in BEM.

The specific request to the churches for "reception" is included in the BEM book itself:

> In support of this process of reception, the Commission would be pleased to know as precisely as possible
>
> — the extent to which your church can recognize in this text the faith of the Church through the ages;
>
> — the consequences your church can draw from this text for its relations and dialogues with other churches, particularly with those churches which also recognize the text as an expression of the apostolic faith;
>
> — the guidance your church can take from this text for its worship, educational, ethical and spiritual life and witness;
>
> — the suggestions your church can make for the ongoing work of Faith and Order as it relates the material of this text on Baptism, Eucharist and Ministry to its long-range research project "Towards the Common Expression of the Apostolic Faith Today."[1]

It is quite clear from these questions that an academic study—though appropriate and for some churches essential—is not what is being requested. Rather, a churchly act at the level of teaching authority is being sought, where possible. Of course, given the diversity of church order, this will take many styles of "reception," from the congregational decision-making style of the free churches to the magisterial style of the episcopally ordered churches. From the directions of the Commission on Faith and Order, reinforced at Vancouver, the churches themselves are being asked to look at this document in light of the apostolic faith through the ages. Popular study will also be an essential part of the spiritual process included in reception.

The opening essay by *William Lazareth*, Director of the Commission on Faith and Order at the time of the reporting out of BEM, is instructive of the Lima Process in the light of Vancouver, within the context of a biblical vision of church unity. His essay provides an indispensable context in which to understand both the process of reception and the development of the BEM text within the whole program and ecclesiology of the Faith and Order movement. It is only by understanding the conciliar fellowship, which is the hope for church reconciliation, that one can understand the role of BEM and the continuing agenda of Faith and Order.[2]

One characteristic of this conference in which these addresses and reports were given was its inclusiveness of a wide array of American church reality. The member churches of the National and World Councils, as well as many churches which do not traditionally relate to the conciliar movement, were represented. This inclusiveness gives witness to the variety of decision-making systems within

---

[1]*Baptism, Eucharist, and Ministry*, Faith and Order Paper 111 (Geneva: World Council of Churches, 1982), Preface, p. x. Note that this may be obtained in the U.S. from Friendship Press, 475 Riverside Dr., New York, NY 10115, for $3.50 plus 15% postage; inquire about bulk rates.

[2]"Ecumenical Chronicle," *The Ecumenical Review* 26 (April, 1974): 291-298; "Conciliar Fellowship," *Mid-stream* 21 (April, 1982): 243-268.

the churches which reflect different theologies of biblical authority and consequently different modes by which the reception process may or may not proceed. A summary of these reception processes and the vision of church they
embody, by *Rastko Trbuhovich*, gives a sense of these presentations and of the
variety of participants. In the conference itself, the churches had a chance to
report on each day, reflecting their design for reception and its theological base
in their church order, their hopes for the utilization of learnings from the conference, and directions for their churches as a result of the challenges presented.
This work will be very important for future Faith and Order study on authority,
deciding together within a conciliar fellowship, and church order. This summary
essay is at the very heart of this collection. While the diversity of responses
gives witness to the richness of American church life, the differences which the
churches brought to the conference make it clear that the process of reception/
rejection is by no means simple. Likewise, it challenges the worldwide ecumenical movement to a sensitivity to that element, particularly in the free-church
tradition in the U.S. context, which is a minority voice within worldwide Christianity. The fact of listening to one another's "reception" processes in itself is
a major ecumenical exercise and will be an opportunity for sharing learnings
about the evangelical witness.

The next essay, by *Edward Kilmartin* of Notre Dame University, outlines a
rich set of historical perspectives from the early church which throw light on
the theology of reception at different moments in history. Spiritual gifts from
one church to another, received in faith, are a characteristic of the Christian
community from the beginning. This essay is particularly helpful for those whose
experience of church life is formed by understandings of reception and decision-
making taken exclusively from American culture. The gravity of the reception
process and its importance for the long-term future of the ecumenical movement
are highlighted by the serious examples drawn from the attempt of the Christian
community to be faithful to its evangelical witness through the ages. Since many
of the examples are taken directly from the conciliar experience, they illuminate
the conciliar fellowship vision on which the Faith and Order study is built.

The essay by *Thomas Hopko* of St. Vladimir's Theological Seminary gives
an introduction to an Orthodox perspective on BEM and its reception. While the
complexity of the Orthodox response reflects the diversity of jurisdictions in the
United States context and throughout the world, his contribution is of unique
importance, given the role of the Orthodox Church in America as the only jurisdiction in the Western hemisphere represented by itself in the Orthodox discussions in the W.C.C. Although this essay does not speak for all Orthodox jurisdictions, it raises questions which are most pertinent to the U.S. environment and
opens challenges to the worldwide experience of Orthodoxy from the U.S. context. *St. Vladimir's Seminary Quarterly* has published a full issue on BEM which
provides a useful amplification of this article.[3]

---

[3]Vol. 27, No. 4 (December, 1983).

In the context of reflecting on the reception processes of the church, the theologians from the Hyde Park area had an opportunity to compare what they had heard from the churches and their reading of the text. *Robert Bertram* has gathered the thoughts of the Hyde Park theologians in the context of his own overview of their contribution. This reflection of theologians provides a model for eliciting similar responses and discussion among traditions working together cooperatively in theological clusters. The collaboration of the church and theological schools as institutions within the ecumenical movement is both modeled and challenged by this conference. Indeed, if the goal of Christian unity is to be realized, the regional and local ecumenical agencies, the academic world, and the polity structures of the communions committed to this vision of church will need to develop models of collaboration. The work of the theologians, the local congregation, and the church bureaucracies needs to be pulled together by professional ecumenists.

The work of BEM is only one element in the long ecumenical process of dialogue being cultivated among the churches who are members of the W.C.C. Commission on Faith and Order. The BEM document follows an affirmation of a view of the church as a conciliar fellowship united in each place and in all places, looking forward to the day when a General Council of the church recognized as such by Orthodox, Catholic, and Protestant can be convened to celebrate the fullness of eucharistic unity and witness with one voice to a suffering and divided world plagued by injustice, hostility, war, and ignorance.

The BEM statement, then, must be seen against the background of the wider ecumenical movement. The next major study of the W.C.C. Commission on Faith and Order, already underway in the Commission of the N.C.C., is "Toward a Common Expression of the Apostolic Faith Today." This study focuses on a wide range of concerns of faith based on the Niceno-Constantinopolitan Creed (381). The article by *Geoffrey Wainwright* of Duke University focuses on this particular study and its relationship to BEM reception and the entire program of Faith and Order. This essay is particularly useful because it outlines in some detail the method developed in the Faith and Order Commission since 1952, focusing on christological rather than comparative ecclesiological theological reflection. It is this essay which makes most clear how it is possible for conservative evangelicals, the Orthodox, confessional and mainline Protestants, and Roman Catholics to move together toward that unity proclaimed in the gospel. Wainwright clarifies the hopes of those theologians representing their churches as they work on explicating the one biblical faith, handed on by the apostles, and confessed in various cultures and contexts throughout the world today.

The N.C.C. Commission on Faith and Order has recently completed a study which contributed to the preparations for Vancouver on the Community of Women and Men in the Church.[4] This study was an important element in all the

---

[4]Janet Crawford and Michael Kinnamon, eds., *In God's Image, Reflections on Identity, Human Wholeness, and the Authority of Scripture* (Geneva: World Council of Churches,

work of the Vancouver Assembly and will continue to be part of the Apostolic Faith Study of the W.C.C. and all the studies undertaken in the N.C.C. Commission on Faith and Order. *Francine Cardman* of Weston Theological School provides a reflection on that study in the context of BEM reception and raises some serious questions which continue to be an important though sometimes weighty part of the ecumenical movement. She stresses the importance of moving beyond the moment when a particular segment of the community is defined as the "problem" to a serious consideration of all the sources available to the christocentric style of Faith and Order and the heritage of the various communions involved.

As part of the context of the worldwide ecumenical movement, the bilateral conversations between churches have become an increasingly rich source of progress in the Faith and Order movement. Many of the member churches of the W.C.C. are in bilateral conversations on the same issues covered by BEM and other W.C.C. studies. For some churches the reception process for the bilaterals is already in progress. For these communions the bilaterals will take precedence over BEM, in that they relate to the specific prospects of deepening communion between two churches. This is particularly important in the context of Anglican/ Roman Catholic relations and of Lutheran/Anglican and Lutheran/Roman Catholic relations at this point in history.

This difference of status and difference of pace sometimes causes tensions in the ecumenical movement. Therefore, the sharing of both these processes in progress and the struggle to relate them is crucial. It is important that they not be seen as competitive—particularly by those whose spirituality does not lend itself to reconciliation. There are learnings to be gained from the processes of reception in place and from the models of steps toward unity being lived out in some of the churches. Likewise, for churches involved in BEM reception, there is a new context in which to study the bilateral and church-union dialogues underway. These processes of reception need to reinforce one another as the reconciling agenda of the church becomes more intense. Similarly, the presence of churches not involved in bilateral dialogue in the BEM process will make it possible for the fruits of the bilateral conversations to have a much wider impact than simply on the two communions which have produced them.

In local and regional study conferences where resources from the bilaterals have made covenanting of congregations and middle judicatories possible, BEM is a new resource for making ecumenical discussion multilateral. This coupling of BEM study and bilateral study has the potential for enriching the conciliar movement at local and regional levels throughout the United States. The N.C.C. Commission on Faith and Order has begun a long-term study of the results of the bilaterals to test the consistency of the results and to help the churches harmonize both their reception processes and their multilateral commitments.

1983); Constance Parvey, ed., *The Community of Women and Men in the Church*, The Sheffield Report (Philadelphia: Fortress Press, 1983).

Furthermore, the contextualizing of these dialogues in the U.S., their communication to the educational system, and their usefulness for the Third World also need to be studied.[5] The essay by *David Willis* of Princeton Theological Seminary raises interesting questions in the context of bilateral and BEM reception.

The church-union negotiations around the world are finding themselves enriched by the text of BEM. At Vancouver many Third World churches spoke appreciatively and enthusiastically about the resource provided by BEM for expediting their churches' movement toward theological consensus. For all ecumenists, the Church of South India has stood as a beacon of hope in the church-union movement. Furthermore, the challenge of a multiplicity of church contexts and specifically the struggles of Third World peoples for their independence in the mid-twentieth century and their human and economic development in our time make the voices of Asia, Africa, and Latin America particularly significant in discussion of the reception of BEM. *Victoria and Russell Chandran* bring decades of experience in the Church of South India to the ecumenical movement. Russell Chandran was a member of the W.C.C. Commission on Faith and Order for two decades from 1952, and Victoria Chandran has served as an educational leader in India and as a prominent proponent of women's roles in the church, both in India and in international ecumenical work. The articles by the Chandrans serve to focus the context of BEM reception in the church-union movement and the Third World in a way which brings the American churches beyond the narrowness of the U.S. and Canadian context.

The rites of baptism and eucharist and the special ordained ministry within the context of the priesthood of all believers were instituted to carry on the mission of the church. Indeed, the tradition handed on by the Apostles, enshrined in the Scripture and in the rites and order of the church, is given to us for mission, for carrying on the one vision of Christ for the world. A world torn by violence, interreligious hatred, and poverty calls the churches to visible unity, to immerse themselves in the concerns of the world as they rise with the Risen Christ from the waters of baptism, and to celebrate the eucharistic banquet as a witness to that unity to which Christ calls the human family.

Finally, a summary essay serves to focus the theological concept of reception most clearly. Written by the chairperson of the N.C.C. Commission on Faith and Order, *William G. Rusch*, it was originally prepared for *Dialog*, in order to assist the Lutheran community as it faces the reception process.

While the enthusiasm of the conference generated a seriousness within the member churches for pursuing their own reception processes, there was also a consistent theme emerging from the discussions: "Documents produced ecumenically should be studied ecumenically." Many of the churches have included

---

[5]*The Bilateral Consultations between the Roman Catholic Church in the United States and Other Christian Communions*, the Catholic Theological Society of America Report of July, 1972; Second Report (1972-1979); Harding Meyer and Lukas Vischer, *Growth in Agreement: Reports and Agreed Statements of Ecumenical Conversations on a World Level* (New York: Paulist Press, 1983).

Christians of other traditions in their reception process at key points. The urgency of the churches' taking their own polity most seriously at this point must be reinforced, but the wider process of spiritual reception will eventually entail reflection on the concerns of BEM with other Christians. While respecting the fact that only those within a church can make decisions at the "highest level of authority," it became clear in discussion that the presence of the dialogue partner was an essential element in "reception." While the text seeks to speak for both those who practice infant baptism and those who baptize only believers, it is difficult to experience the full witness of those with the different practice without the human presence in dialogue. While the text assures congregational and presbyterial churches that the personal episcopate need not diminish collegiality and participation, the witness of a bishop from a united church can give presbyterial or congregational living testimony to the richness these diverse witnesses can provide within one church.

Toward the end of the conference a short recommendation was passed by the representatives of the churches to be shared with those concerned:

October 14, 1983

To Whom It May Concern:

The undersigned attended a Conference on the Churches' Reception of the Baptism-Eucharist-Ministry document of the World Council of Churches' Faith and Order Commission from October 12-14, 1983 at the Lutheran School of Theology at Chicago. Many of us were delegated by our national offices to attend this Conference; all of us tried to speak out of our own traditions in faithful witness to the enriching variety of God's Church.

One of the convictions and conclusions to which we came through dialogue is that this document should be studied and prayed over locally in *ecumenical groups* as well as single-church alignments. We therefore commend to our churches this method of considering and using the document at appropriate levels of church life, but especially in judicatories and congregations. We pray that this will be done, and would be glad to help the process in any way possible to us.

In conclusion it is important to recognize that the Commission on Faith and Order has provided considerable resources for the study of BEM, materials available for individuals and seminaries as well as for those churches formally involved in the reception process.[6] The text itself is much like a Zen painting with faint and skillful lines; however, the reality of the form is what does not appear. The great heritage of the Christian tradition and the theological developments of the

---

[6]William Lazareth, *Growing Together in Baptism, Eucharist, and Ministry* (Geneva: World Council of Churches, 1982), $3.95; Max Thurian, ed., *Ecumenical Perspectives on Baptism, Eucharist, and Ministry*, Faith and Order Paper 116 (Geneva: World Council of

church through the centuries are not there and can only be seen as one looks through the lines of convergence outlined in BEM to the other traditions with whom one is in dialogue. Likewise, the new experiences of churches who did not themselves give rise to the historical divisions, churches in the Third World, also fill these gaps. These new contexts and experiences, those of lay piety, the new and emerging roles of women, and churches whose struggles find the heritage of old-world divisions intolerable, will fill out this sketch with the rich celebration of the Christian faith to which a common understanding of baptism, eucharist, and ministry points us.

It is hoped that this text might be a "fragile bridge of words" by which we can reach one another's faith life and enrich each other's own understanding of the one gospel of Jesus Christ through increased study, prayer, collaboration, and theological research toward the unity of Christ's body which is at the center of the life of Christian faith. This consultation raised most forcefully the question of whether it is possible to understand Jesus Christ as the Life of the World, without recognizing that he stands over the church.

Churches, 1983), $10.90; Max Thurian and Geoffrey Wainwright, eds., *Baptism and Eucharist: Ecumenical Convergence in Celebration* (Geneva: World Council of Churches, 1983), $10.90; *Towards Visible Unity*, Volume I: *Minutes and Addresses*, Faith and Order Paper 112; Volume II: *Study Papers and Reports*, Faith and Order Paper 113 (Geneva: World Council of Churches, 1982). The first three are available from the address in n. 1, above, at the prices indicated, plus 15% postage.

BAPTISM, EUCHARIST, AND MINISTRY UPDATE

William Lazareth

I wish to analyze Lima-1982 against the broad ecclesiastical background of Vancouver-1983 and within the even broader ecclesiological vision of John 17. My twofold rationale: (1) updating *Baptism, Eucharist, and Ministry* (hereafter, BEM) can best be done highlighting excerpts from its most authoritative ecumenical commentary to date—namely, Vancouver's Issue-Two Report on "Taking Steps toward Unity"; and (2) predating BEM is certainly even more important, if it is now to be launched into ecumenical orbit as our authentic common witness to the faith of the church catholic. Basically it is not a crisis of mind but a crisis of will that we now face together. Our integrated constituency represents at once both the present problem and the potential solution. How can the professors and the confessors, the scholars and the church leaders, the *periti* and the *magisterium*, those with the "know-what" and those with the "know-how" begin to think and pray and speak the truth in love together in order to enable the whole people of God to grapple with some of the essential features of the *sensus fidelium* in our common quest for ecumenical renewal in both church unity and church mission?

Allowing for some ecumenical exaggeration to make the point, we might well say that Faith and Order has brought the churches—all the churches—to a moment of truth. The impressive results of decades of ecumenical scholarship dedicated to the reconciliation of the churches' unfaith now also serve ironically to expose its corollary disorder. We have moved symbolically from the doctrinal kitchen to the juridical dining room. Having prepared a banquet that is widely hailed to be as doctrinally nutritious as it is ecclesially palatable, the professorial cooks have suddenly posed the unprecedented challenge of how much our hier-

William Henry Lazareth (Lutheran Church in America) is presently pastor of Holy Trinity Lutheran Church in New York City, and Distinguished Visiting Professor at the Lutheran Theological Seminary in Philadelphia. From 1980 to 1983, he was director of the Faith and Order Secretariat of the World Council of Churches in Geneva, after serving as director of the Dept. for Church in Society of the Lutheran Church in America's Division for Mission in N. America (1976-1980), and for two decades before that as Hagan Professor of Systematic Theology and Dean of Faculty at the Lutheran Theological Seminary in Philadelphia. He has a B.A. from Princeton University, an M.Div. from the Philadelphia Lutheran Seminary, and a Ph.D. from Columbia University/Union Theological Seminary (1958). His fellowships have taken him to the Universities of Tübingen, Lund, and Pennsylvania. Most recent of his dozen books are *Growing Together in Baptism, Eucharist, and Ministry* (W.C.C., 1982) and *Present Your Bodies: Worship and Witness in Romans* (L.C.A. Board of Publication, 1983). Editor of another thirteen books, the most recent include the BEM text and *Lord of Life: Theological Explorations* (both W.C.C., 1983). His articles, essays, and reviews have appeared in a wide variety of books and journals. He has preached and lectured in a large number of Lutheran and ecumenical settings, and paid official visits to leaders of many major Christian bodies around the world.

archical customers in the ecumenical restaurant are able to order and willing to swallow. Moreover, there are potentially some very high denominational costs in consuming such rich ecumenical fare, not least in view of the suspected invalidity of many of our long-expired denominational credit cards.

Our bilateral and multilateral dialogue representatives are returning to their sponsoring home communions with convergences that no one dared anticipate. Often they reveal the doctrinal reality that our theological differences no longer correspond to our denominational labels. They also expose a paradoxical juridical reality. On the one hand, some of our so-called "high church" communions have absolutely no governing canonical guidance for dealing authoritatively with doctrinal materials admittedly co-authored by theologians representing other communions which are still officially anathametized or condemned as either heretical or schismatic. On the other hand, others of our so-called "low church" communions have absolutely no magisterial apparatus for officially determining what is, or what is not, the authentic faith of the church "once for all delivered to the saints," to say nothing of having any *episkope* authority able to make such official declarations with binding authority for the beliefs of the faithful.

Canonically, "to receive" is the highest form of church reaction, while parliamentarily "to receive" is precisely the lowest. This is our challenge and opportunity: the eager doctrinal hens have come home to roost among very nervous and inexperienced juridical roosters, and no one is quite sure just how much egg is going to end up on whose face!

On a more serious level, reflecting Faith and Order's ecclesial piety and commitment, I want to integrate (1) an updating of Lima-1982 by Vancouver-1983 with (2) our predating of Lima-1982 in the High Priestly Prayer of our Lord as formulated in the seventeenth chapter of the Fourth Gospel. I know that it is hermeneutically invalid to look to John 17 for ecclesiastical *directives* to sinfully divided churches for whom it was never written. However, I also believe that this Word of God does provide some ecclesiological *direction* for guiding our holy calling to manifest the visible unity of the one, holy, catholic, and apostolic body of the incarnate, crucified, and risen Lord, Jesus, the Christ of God. Allow me, then, to initiate our critical BEM reception these upcoming days and years by highlighting Vancouver-1983 in fidelity to John 17. You will recall John's presentation of Christ's three-part prayer in which he prays for himself, then for his nearest disciples, the apostles, and finally, for us within the church universal.

First, we recall the words of Christ's prayer for himself:

> When Jesus had spoken these words, he lifted up his eyes to heaven
> and said: "Father, the hour has come; glorify thy Son that the Son
> may glorify thee, since thou hast given him power over all flesh, to
> give eternal life to all whom thou hast given him. And this is eternal
> life, that they know thee the only true God, and Jesus Christ whom
> thou hast sent. I glorified thee on earth, having accomplished the
> work which thou gavest me to do; and now, Father, glorify thou me

in thy own presence with the glory which I had with thee before the
world was made. . . . And for their sake I consecrate myself, that
they also may be consecrated in truth." (Jn. 17:1-5, 19)

Here I want to stress that, as Jesus anticipated the morrow of his death, he
unequivocally identified his earthly humiliation as the foretaste of his heavenly
glorification. Biblical scholars inform us that the Greek word translated here as
"consecrate" means "dedicate a sacrifice for the service of God." Nowhere is
this term ever used outside the Bible. In the Old Testament, "consecrate" is
used to depict the sacrifice of things by Abraham, by Israel, by the priesthood
of Aaron. Only in the New Testament does Jesus alone declare, "I consecrate
myself," as the salvific ground for the fulfillment of Yahweh's gracious purposes
for humankind. In the midst of many other, ancillary, and even specious descrip-
tions of the calling of the ecumenical movement in the world today, I wish to
attest to this Christ-centered understanding of church unity that prevails unqual-
ifiedly in the Faith and Order movement.

"It is Jesus Christ and him crucified" who is confessed to be at the heart
of the ecumenical goal of church unity. I will try to illustrate that claim by some
excerpts from the Vancouver-1983 text on "Taking Steps toward Unity," in
which the Lordship of Jesus Christ governs our vision of the ecumenical goal:

I. The goal: Church unity as a credible sign and witness

1. Our central ecumenical goal is acknowledged in the World
Council of Churches' first purpose and function: "To call the
churches to the goal of visible unity in one faith and in one eucharistic fellowship expressed in worship and in common life in Christ,
and to advance towards that unity in order that the world may
believe." This single vision unites our two profoundest ecumenical
concerns: the unity and renewal of the Church and the healing and
destiny of the human community. Church unity is vital to the health
of the Church and to the future of the human family. Moreover, it
is a response of obedience to God's will and an offering of praise to
God's glory.

2. Earlier gatherings have perceived and stressed various aspects
of this vision. The churches at Amsterdam (1948) said "We intend
to stay together" in their journey towards that goal. The Evanston
Assembly (1954) discerned in Jesus Christ the only hope which can
motivate such a journey. New Delhi (1961) emphasized that this
unity means "all in each place as one fully committed fellowship".
Montreal (1963) spoke of the primary source of such unity: "the
Tradition of the Gospel testified in scripture, transmitted in and by
the Church through the power of the Holy Spirit". Uppsala (1968)
lifted up the catholicity and diversity of true unity.

3. Nairobi (1975) attempted to gather up many of these themes
in a way which emphasizes the universality of the goal:

> The one Church is to be envisioned as a conciliar fellowship
> of local churches which are themselves truly united. In this
> conciliar fellowship, each local church possesses, in com-
> munion with the others, the fullness of catholicity, witnesses
> to the same apostolic faith, and therefore recognizes the
> others as belonging to the same Church of Christ and
> guided by the same Spirit . . . They are bound together
> because they have received the same baptism and share in
> the same eucharist; they recognize each other's members
> and ministries. They are one in their common commitment
> to confess the Gospel of Christ by proclamation and service
> to the world. To this end, each church aims at maintain-
> ing sustained and sustaining relationships with her sister
> churches, expressed in conciliar gatherings whenever re-
> quired for the fulfillment of their common calling.

This view of the goal clearly will and should be further developed.

4. It is the implication of such Church unity for the destiny of
the human community—an implication clearly contained in earlier
statements but not so clearly expressed—which has impressed this
Vancouver Assembly. Peace and justice, on the one hand, baptism,
eucharist and ministry, on the other, have claimed our attention.
They belong together. Indeed the aspect of Christian unity which
has been most striking to us here in Vancouver is that of a *eucharistic vision*. Christ—the life of the world—unites heaven and earth, God
and world, spiritual and secular. His body and blood, given us in the
elements of bread and wine, integrate liturgy and diaconate, proclamation and acts of healing. "The remembrance of Christ is the very
content of the preached word as it is of the eucharistic meal, each
reinforces the other. The celebration of the eucharist properly includes the proclamation of the word" (BEM, Eucharist, 12). Our
eucharistic vision thus encompasses the whole reality of Christian
worship, life and witness, and tends—when truly discovered—to shed
new light on Christian unity in its full richness of diversity. It also
sharpens the pain of our present division at the table of the Lord;
but in bringing forth the organic unity of Christian commitment and
of its unique source in the incarnate self-sacrifice of Christ, the
eucharistic vision provides us with new and inspiring guidance on
our journey towards a full and credible realization of our given
unity.

II. Marks of such a witnessing unity

5. Such a strong Church unity, affirmed in words, lived in
deeds, relevant and credible to the problems of human community,
would properly have at least three marks which the divided churches
do not yet fully share.

6. First, the churches would share a common understanding of
the apostolic faith, and be able to confess this Message together in

ways understandable, reconciling and liberating to their contempo-
raries. Living this apostolic faith together, the churches help the
world to realize God's design for creation.

7. Second, confessing the apostolic faith together, the churches
would share a full mutual recognition of baptism, the eucharist and
ministry, and be able through their visible communion to let the
healing and uniting power of these gifts become more evident amidst
the divisions of humankind.

8. Third, the churches would agree on common ways of decision-making and ways of teaching authoritatively, and be able to
demonstrate qualities of communion, participation and corporate
responsibility which could shed healing light in a world of conflict.

9. Such a unity—overcoming church division, binding us together in the face of racism, sexism, injustice—would be a witnessing
unity, a credible sign of the new creation.[1]

I turn next to our Lord's prayer for his closest of the disciples—the apostles.

"I have given them thy word; and the world has hated them because
they are not of the world, even as I am not of the world. I do not
pray that thou shouldst take them out of the world, but that thou
shouldst keep them from the evil one. They are not of the world,
even as I am not of the world. Sanctify them in the truth; thy word
is truth. As thou didst send me into the world, so I have sent them
into the world."((Jn. 17:14-18)

With regard to the unique role of the apostles in the ministry of the church of
Jesus Christ, major advances have been made recently in the realization of our
ecumenical goal. Ecumenism has moved beyond pan-Protestantism to benefit
from the eucharistic and conciliar treasures of the Orthodox and Roman Catholic communions. The major difference in BEM between the Accra penultimate
text and the Lima ultimate text lies in the richer development of the apostolic
Tradition. Our earlier preoccupation with ecumenism in space is more appropriately balanced by an ecumenism in time in which the uniqueness of the apostolic
period is now venerated by the people of God as foundational for all that the
later people of God say and do. This apostolic authority rests in the uniqueness
of that which was vouchsafed "once for all"—to the saints of the early church,
and that is something for which I as a Protestant Christian, an evangelical catholic, wish to pay public homage.

Therefore, when it now comes time after Vancouver to take concrete steps
toward the realization of our ecumenical goal, increasingly the stress is given to
the interdependence of the two foci of (1) mutual recognition of ministers and
ministries, and (2) the fullness of the church's confession of the apostolic faith.

---

[1]David Gill, ed., *Gathered for Life: Official Report—VI Assembly, World Council of
Churches, Vancouver, Canada, 24 July-10 August, 1983* (Geneva: World Council of Churches;
Grand Rapids: Wm. B. Eerdmans, 1983), "Taking Steps towards Unity," pp. 43-45.

Indeed, we were able to get where we got in BEM only because we repudiated the prevailing comparative ecclesiological methodology. In the one Christian tree, no longer did the branches and twigs articulate how different they were from each other. Convergences emerged only when the twigs and branches tried commonly to describe their same apostolic, patristic trunk. Consequently, a first major step proposed at Vancouver-1983 was an evaluation of the doctrinal results through the process of reception of BEM by the churches:

11. "Baptism, Eucharist and Ministry" is at one and the same time a challenge and an opportunity for the churches. For the first time the various traditions are challenged to face each other not simply on the basis of their own identities, but in the presence of a common attempt to express a convergent statement of the apostolic faith. This text is grounded in that "Tradition of the Gospel" of which Montreal spoke. Confronted with this text, the churches are called to express in what measure they can recognize *together* the same apostolic faith. The document invites our churches to make the journey from isolated identities towards fuller fellowship. We receive this invitation with real excitement, but also with a realization that despite its achievements, "Baptism, Eucharist and Ministry" falls short of convergence on some important issues. The pain which this causes will be felt on our journey.

12. The terminology we must use in this process of reception differs in various churches, and it is not possible or proper for the WCC to prescribe official definitions. But it may be helpful to suggest the following:

13. In speaking of "Baptism, Eucharist and Ministry" as a "convergent statement", we do not imply that full agreement has already been reached. Rather, we speak of a statement which arises out of diverse ways of expressing the same faith, but which points to a common life and understanding not yet fully attained or expressed. Nevertheless, this unity remains the goal of the ecumenical task. These expressions "bend towards each other". These convergences give assurance that despite a diversity of traditions the churches have much in common in their understanding of the faith. The "Baptism, Eucharist and Ministry" text, however, is not yet a "consensus statement", meaning by that term "that experience of life and articulation of faith necessary to realize and maintain the Church's visible unity" (BEM Preface, ix).

14. It is also important to distinguish the "process of reception" and the "official response". The "official response", which is requested at a relatively early date, is intended to initiate a process of study and communication in which each church will attempt to provide an answer to the four preface questions, answers which are not simply the response of individuals or groups within the church but which, in some sense, understood by the church itself, are given on behalf of the church. This "official response" is explicitly not

understood to be the church's ultimate decisions about "Baptism, Eucharist and Ministry", but rather the initial step in a longer process of reception. This "process of reception" is something which each church will have to understand in terms of its own tradition; it refers generally, however, to the long-range process by which the churches seek to recognize the one apostolic faith in and through the words of the text and freshly to lay hold of the new life which that faith promises. This process is thus often spoken of as a "spiritual process of reception", and it will require much time and wide participation at various levels of the life of the church: congregations, theological faculties and ecumenical commissions, and ecclesiastical authorities. Additional ecumenical consultations may be helpful. We emphasize the importance of this "spiritual process of reception". The measure of our participation in this spiritual pilgrimage is at the same time an indication of the quality of our reception. It is clear that the meaning of the term "reception", since it is now used with respect to churches in a divided situation, varies somewhat from, but does not contradict, the usage of the early centuries.[2]

By way of concrete illustration, it means that you do not go home and measure Lima in terms of the Council of Trent or the Augsburg Confession or the Thirty-Nine Articles. We are reversing the order and asking, "How do you validate your communion's articulation of its faith in light of the *paradosis* of the *kerygma*, the holy Tradition of the gospel?" So, for example, if there is any incompatibility between BEM and the fifth article of the Augsburg Confession on "the Ministry," it may be so much the worse for the Augsburg Confession.

Here we may all find help in Faith and Order's Fourth World Conference in Montreal-1963, which made a clear distinction between the "Tradition" and "the traditions."[3] It proved helpful to differentiate between "Tradition," meaning the gospel itself transmitted from generation to generation in and by the church, and "traditions," meaning the churches' diverse expressions of the one Tradition. This distinction made possible a more dynamic view of Tradition and its relation to Scripture. "Tradition" was accordingly understood not as a sum of tenets fixed once for all time and transmitted mechanically from generation to generation but, rather, as a living reality, God's revelation in Christ, and its course throughout history. In other words, God's revelation in the past is accessible today only as Tradition.

To quote perhaps the best known words of the Montreal Faith and Order report: "We exist as Christians by the Tradition of the Gospel, the *paradosis* of the *kerygma*, testified in Scripture, transmitted in and by the Church through the power of the Holy Spirit." This Tradition comes to us in the form

---

[2]Ibid., pp. 45-47.
[3]See Introduction of Ellen Flesseman-van Leer, ed., *The Bible: Its Authority and Interpretation in the Ecumenical Movement.* Faith and Order Paper 99 (Geneva: World Council of Churches, 1980).

of our confessional traditions. The question arises, therefore, as to whether and to what extent the various traditions are embodiments of *the* Tradition; i.e., whether and to what extent they faithfully transmit revelation. The Montreal report then points to the Scriptures. The Bible is, as it were, Tradition written down at a decisive early stage in its course through the ages. In the words of the report, "The criterion for the genuine Tradition is to be found in the holy scriptures rightly interpreted." Significantly, the report recognizes that Tradition and Scripture are not two independent entities. They are so intertwined that neither one of them, taken in itself, can simply be used as authoritative.

On the one hand, the Reformation principle of *sola scriptura* is qualified by the reminder that the Bible is part of Tradition and embedded in Tradition; in fact, it becomes living Tradition as it is rightly interpreted in ever new situations. On the other hand, Tradition as source of revelation is qualified by the assertion that it is only accessible in traditions whose trustworthiness must be tested in the light of Scripture. One of the most far-reaching differences between the "protestant" and "catholic" views is being bridged by this double qualification. The weight of this rapprochement is all the greater since the Faith and Order Conference at Montreal (1963) was the first one in which the Orthodox churches fully participated and in which the Roman Catholic tradition began to be represented. That report received wide recognition and had a certain influence on the formation of the Dogmatic Constitution on Divine Revelation of Vatican II. In short, many of our church traditions which have long since disavowed fundamentalism when it comes to dealing hermeneutically with the Scripture do not yet have a comparable art when it comes to dealing with the historical documents of the articulated dogma of the church in question. And that is something to which many will have to contribute in the months and years ahead in the BEM reception process.

It was also felt necessary at Vancouver-1983 that we take a closely related second step. Along with moving toward the mutual recognition of ministers and ministries, there is also a need for a common understanding of the apostolic faith. Actually we backed into BEM because those three issues happen to be among the most neuralgic points in the interrelationships among the communions. Obviously one does not confess the creed by beginning with the middle of the third article. If this sacramental doctrine is to enjoy apostolic integrity, its truncated ecclesiology must be linked organically with a fully orbed trinitarian faith. Only then could it serve to validate the kind of mutual trust which will be necessary for the calling of a truly authentic universal council. That is why the limited goals of BEM are the interim steps of mutual recognition of ministers and ministries, rather than the final step of organic church union.

Therefore, parallel with the churches' reception in whatever form of the BEM texts, the Commission will move on to plumb the depths of the apostolic faith. Vancouver declared:

18. Reception of "Baptism, Eucharist and Ministry" clearly implies this further step, for *what* the churches are asked to receive in this text is not simply a document, but *in* this document the apostolic faith from which it comes, and to which it bears witness. Nairobi (1975) strongly recommended that: ". . . the churches . . . undertake a common effort to receive, reappropriate and confess together, as contemporary occasion requires, the Christian truth and faith, delivered through the apostles and handed down through the centuries. Such common action, arising from free and inclusive discussion under the commonly acknowledged authority of God's word, must aim both to clarify and to embody the unity and the diversity which are proper to the Church's life and mission."

19. As this effort has begun to take shape—its first fruits are still several years ahead of us—it has become clear that any common attempt by the churches to express that faith which unites all contemporary churches and all believers of all ages with the apostolic Church would need to be conceived along three lines: first, a common recognition of the apostolic faith as expressed in creeds of the undivided Church such as the Apostolic Symbol and especially the Nicene Creed; second, a common explication of the faith so recognized in terms understandable today; and third, a common confession by the churches today of that same apostolic faith in relation to the contemporary challenges to the Gospel.

20. Such an achievement is obviously beyond the reach of any commission document or WCC action. It could only be an event, given by God and received by the churches themselves—perhaps such an event as the Nairobi description of conciliar fellowship envisioned. Nevertheless, such an event can be hoped and prayed for, and the project "Towards the Common Expression of the Apostolic Faith Today" offers a beginning towards such an event. It will be impossible to take this common step if in this study of the apostolic faith we do not give special attention to the nature and mystery of the Church of God, since the confession of the one, holy, catholic and apostolic Church belongs to the apostolic faith.[4]

By way of brief conclusion, we may recall those words in Christ's High Priestly Prayer which in this century have probably become the foremost articulation of the ecumenical motto:

"I do not pray for these only, but also for those who believe in me through their word, that they may all be one; even as thou, Father, art in me, and I in thee, that they also may be in us, so that the world may believe that thou has sent me." (Jn. 17:20-21)

Whether or not this prayer is realized in history will probably depend on whether or not we are able to be faithful *simultaneously* to the two foci articulated in its

---

[4]Gill, *Gathered for Life*, pp. 48-49.

final part: The first focus, the visible unity toward which the presently divided churches aspire, is not merely a matter of clever ecclesial diplomats getting together, trading adverbs, and coming up with the least-worst compromise as the ground for their institutional survival. Ultimately, the unity to which we aspire is the unity which we confess. It is not a matter of our manufacturing church unity; it is a matter of manifesting that unity in which the church itself shares by virtue of its being incorporated through baptism into the Christ who is one with the Father. This baptism is the only exegetically defensible ground for the ecumenical movement.

The second focus of this concluding passage is clearly the calling of the church in fulfilling God's ultimate purpose: the redemption of all creation. The totality of reality is what the Creator is after, working through the church as the faithful instrument of God's redemptive love. Consequently, the third major step which was recommended at Vancouver-1983 was the necessity of helping our churches to explore and express more clearly the relation between the unity of the church and the renewal of human community.

> 21. At this Assembly we have sensed a tension between some of those who are concerned with the unity of the Church and others concerned with the desperate need for justice, peace and reconciliation in the human community. For some, the search for a unity in one faith and one eucharistic fellowship seems, at best secondary, at worst irrelevant to the struggles for peace, justice and human dignity; for others the Church's political involvement against the evils of history seems, at best, secondary, at worst detrimental to its role as eucharistic community and witness to the Gospel.
>
> 22. As Christians we want to affirm there can be no such division between unity and human renewal, either in the Church or in the agenda of the WCC. Indeed, the "Baptism, Eucharist and Ministry" text has underlined for us that baptism, eucharist and ministry are healing and uniting signs of a Church living and working for a renewed and reconciled humankind.
>
>> As they grow in the Christian life of faith, baptized believers demonstrate that humanity can be regenerated and liberated . . . Likewise, they acknowledge that baptism, as a baptism into Christ's death, has ethical implications which not only call for personal sanctification, but also motivate Christians to strive for the realization of the will of God in all realms of life (Rom. 6:9ff; Gal. 3:27-28; 1 Pet. 2:21, 4:6).
>
> 23. In the same way, the text on the eucharist expressly endorses a kind of eucharistic life-style in the midst of all struggles for justice, peace and freedom in today's world:
>
>> The eucharist embraces all aspects of life. It is a representative act of thanksgiving and offering on behalf of the whole

world . . . All kinds of injustice, racism, separation and lack of freedom are radically challenged when we share in the body and blood of Christ. Through the eucharist the all-renewing grace of God penetrates and restores human personality and dignity.

24. Similarly, through the study on the Community of Women and Men in the Church, many have discovered that life in unity must carry with it the overcoming of division between the sexes, and have begun to envision what profound changes must take place in the life of the Church and the world. The participants at the Sheffield conference on the Community of Women and Men in the Church emphasized that one form of oppression is interwoven with others. The inter-relatedness of racism, classism and sexism calls for a combined struggle since no one form of renewal will, by itself, accomplish a renewal of ecclesial community. Such insights should be deepened and built upon with the study on the Unity of the Church and the Renewal of Human Community. Further, the specific challenges contained in the Sheffield recommendations should be taken up in the process of response to "Baptism, Eucharist and Ministry", the work on confessing the apostolic faith, and the quest for common ways of decision-making and teaching authoritatively.

25. As we have explored together the relation between God's Church and God's world, we have been struck by Uppsala's affirmation that "the Church is bold in speaking of itself as the sign of the coming unity of humankind". At Vancouver we have been challenged to deepen our understanding of what we mean when we make such a bold claim. Thus we propose that the Faith and Order Commission make a theological exploration of the Church as "sign" a central part of its programme on the Unity of the Church and the Renewal of Human Community. This recommendation implies our conviction that the Church is called to be a prophetic "sign", a prophetic community through which and by which the transformation of the world can take place. It is only a church which goes out from its eucharistic centre, strengthened by word and sacrament and thus strengthened in its own identity, resolved to become what it is, that it can take the world on to its agenda. There never will be a time when the world, with all its political, social and economic issues, ceases to be the agenda of the Church. At the same time, the Church can go out to the edges of society, not fearful of being distorted or confused by the world's agenda, but confident and capable of recognizing that God is already there.[5]

I conclude with a personal testimony of hope. In reporting on his visit to Istanbul and relations with the Holy Orthodox Church, Pope John Paul II pointed out what appears to be a major redirection in the course of Christian

---

[5]Ibid., pp. 49-50.

history. He said: "The second millennium witnessed our progressive separation. The opposite movement has begun everywhere. It is necessary, and I beseech the Father of lights from whom every perfect gift comes down, to grant that the dawn of the third millennium shall rise on our full refound communion."[6] Perhaps that pious hope for full communion between Roman Catholics and Orthodox might somehow providentially also be extended to all other separated Christians in the not-doo-distant future. So, in a special way we commend Christian ecumenism to God's favor. While resolving not to slacken in the efforts required of us, we know that the unity which we seek is finally a gift of God the Spirit to God's people. Only God will allow us to advance in fulfillment of Christ's supreme desire—*Ut unum sint*.

---

[6]*Origins*, vol. 10, no. 24 (November 27, 1980).

SUMMARY OF U.S. CHURCHES'
BEM RECEPTION PROCESSES

Rastko Trbuhovich

An important element of the Chicago Conference on BEM Reception, October 12-14, 1983, was the detailed sharing among the church "teams" of their reception processes. Two opportunities were given to the churches to offer information. First, the Commission on Faith and Order of the National Council of Churches of Christ sent questionnaires to the ecumenical officers of the communions soliciting basic information on the reception process. The returned questionnaires were made available to conference participants. The second opportunity was the plenary on the first day of the conference devoted to reports by the teams on the subject of "Reception as Teams Understand It." The summaries below of the communions' reception processes are taken from these two sources.

The distinction between "receiving" BEM and "responding" was not clear for many. The conference program served a valuable purpose in clarifying this distinction. However, even where the distinction was perceived, the detailed process outlined was focused almost exclusively on the response. It is apparent that the response is much more easily planned than the reception. The directions and consequences of reception will begin to make themselves clear only after the churches are well into the study processes planned for BEM, only after some "digestion."

The invitation from the World Council of Churches' Faith and Order Commission to all the churches to respond officially to BEM "at the highest appropriate level of authority" set in motion a variety of processes indigenous to the various ways in which the Christian churches in the United States are ordered. The "appropriate level" of response for the most episcopally ordered churches is from the bishops themselves. The highest level of authority for many of the free churches is none other than the individual congregation, thus making a single, representative response from these communions provisional. The majority of the churches fall somewhere along the spectrum between these two points, with connectional systems investing a variously constituted periodic General Assembly, Conference, Convention, or Synod with appropriate legislative authority.

Team members from some free churches could not merely relate details of the mechanics of their BEM study and response processes. Conference participants had to hear that major elements of BEM—the sacraments of baptism and

Rastko Trbuhovich (Serbian Orthodox) is a consultant to the Commission on Faith and Order of the National Council of the Church of Christ in the U.S.A., and also serves as a parish priest. From 1974 till 1981, he served as Secretary of the Serbian Orthodox Diocese of Eastern America and Canada (Edgeworth, PA). He holds a B.A. from Iona College, New Rochelle, NY, and an M.Div. from St. Vladimir's Orthodox Theological Seminary, Scarsdale, NY.

eucharist, or the ordained threefold ministry—were elements totally foreign to their self-experience as Christian churches. The feeling of having one's Christian witness excluded from BEM, or the difficulty of changing practices which are fundamental to the identity of a church, were heard and felt. These are the inevitable pains for all in the ecumenical movement.

Summaries of Reception Processes

The Roman Catholic Church. The R.C.C. is a member of the W.C.C. Faith and Order Commission and participated in the formulation of BEM. Rome will not "receive" BEM, but it will "respond" officially, itself a recognition of the importance of the Lima statement. Reception cannot be accomplished alone but in conjunction with other churches to lead to a change in relations among the churches. The bishops are the official teachers (*magisterium*) of the R.C.C. The request to receive BEM raises questions as to how the essential teaching role of the bishops relates to the wider popular reception of teaching and how the *magisterium* can authoritatively accept a teaching. The Secretariat for the Promotion of Christian Unity in Rome is officially in charge of the response process for the R.C.C. They will seek input from the R.C.C. around the world by mid-1985 in order to formulate the official response. In the U.S., study of the document is being conducted by a research team of the Catholic Theological Society of America, by theological faculties, and by some dioceses. The National Association of Diocesan Ecumenical Officers is encouraging local ecumenical study of BEM. The study process may be extended beyond the current limited participation.

The Armenian Church of America. For the Armenian Church, reception of BEM requires serious examination in terms of the apostolic faith, taking into consideration the dialogues of the Armenian Church with both Roman Catholics and Eastern Orthodox. Reception by the Armenians implies consideration of the attitudes and needs of all the dioceses throughout the world. It will involve the bishops, the Synod, and the Patriarch of all Armenians in Etchmiadzin, Armenia, USSR. The response process is being directed by the Patriarchate, but the details of the American diocese's involvement in this process have not been made clear at this time.

The Greek Orthodox Archdiocese in North and South America. (The Archdiocese was not represented at the Chicago conference but did provide the following information.) The Archdiocese is a member of the W.C.C. through the Ecumenical Patriarchate of Constantinople. The reception process is being conducted by a special synodical committee in Istanbul, and the Archdiosese will be given opportunity to contribute recommendations to this committee. Greek

Orthodox theologians are participating in the BEM study being conducted by the Orthodox Theological Society in America.

The Orthodox Church in America. Reception for the O.C.A. will be affirming what it finds in BEM of its own faith and life, identifying and explaining that which it cannot affirm, and accepting the judgement of BEM where practice is not in accord with the faith.[1] The Holy Synod of Bishops of the O.C.A. will formulate the official evaluation and response to BEM, which will be doctrinally and canonically authoritative. The response will be made in the context of the dogmatic and sacramental unity of the universal Orthodox Church. The reception process is guided by the Department of External Affairs, chaired by Fr. John Meyendorff (Fr. Leonid Kishkovsky, Secretary), with assistance from the Task Force on Ecumenism and a special theological task force on BEM. The study process has not been fully detailed yet, but it will include study by the theological schools and the preparation of a study guide for parish use. The O.C.A. is participating in the study of BEM by the Orthodox Theological Society of America, the results of which will be incorporated into the respective study processes of several local Orthodox churches.

The United Methodist Church. The reception process for the United Methodist Church, now being implemented by the General Commission on Christian Unity and Interreligious Concerns, involves grassroots study groups in fifteen to twenty local churches and a special twelve-person task force of theologians, clergy, laity, and church professionals. The basis for both study groups will be the Lima document and the study guide by William Lazareth. The staff of the General Commission will receive the reports of both study components and meld the two together. The General Commission or its Executive Committee will meet to review the composite report and forward it to the Council of Bishops for consideration and action in September, 1985. The bishops, who will have completed their own study of the Lima statement, will be free to choose between their own conclusions and the report received from the General Commission or to combine them. The General Conference, a legislative and not a programmatic body, is being asked in 1984 to support the study and response plan, particularly by "urg[ing] local churches and other units at every level of the denomination to explore the incorporation of the theological convergence into its worship, educational, ethical, spiritual life and witness. . . ."[2] The final report will be received from the Council of Bishops by the General Commission and transmitted to the W.C.C. on behalf of the United Methodist Church by December 31, 1985.

[1] A special issue of *St. Vladimir's Theological Quarterly* addresses Orthodox concerns relative to BEM, vol. 27, no. 4 (December, 1983).
[2] Petition to the 1984 General Conference of the United Methodist Church, General Commission on Christian Unity and Interreligious Concerns; Robert Huston, General Secretary.

The African Methodist Episcopal Church. (The A.M.E. Church was not represented at the Chicago conference but did provide some information.) The reception process will be directed by the Council of Bishops, who will instruct several of the church's theologians to study BEM and present a critical review for consideration by the Council. The status and potential use of the document are yet to emerge from the study process. All documents intended for general church instruction and teaching will need acceptance by the General Conference, the highest legislative body for the A.M.E. Church. Its next meeting is July, 1984.

The African Methodist Episcopal Zion Church. BEM has not been discussed enough within the A.M.E. Zion Church for an understanding or process of reception to develop. There is little hope that the General Conference, the highest legislative authority, will be prepared at its 1984 meeting to resolve the question of the reception of BEM for the church. More realistically, it may provide some direction for a serious study of BEM which would conclude with a resolution by the 1988 General Conference.

The Christian Methodist Episcopal Church. (The C.M.E. Church provided information on its BEM reception process, although it was unable to be represented at the Chicago conference.) The reception process for the C.M.E. Church is being directed by its General Board of Christian Education. The details of the process have not been formalized but include study of the document on various levels, including participation in ecumenical forums. The General Board of Christian Education must affirm the document and refer it to the General Connectional Board, which in turn submits it to the quadrennial meeting of the General Conference (next meeting in 1986). However, once the General Board of Christian Education has affirmed the document, which appears very likely, it becomes part of the program of ministry for the C.M.E. Church.

The Episcopal Church. The Episcopal Church has an established process for receiving agreements achieved through bilateral and multilateral dialogues, which involves thorough study of the document at the local, seminary, and diocesan levels, and, wherever possible, persons from the other communion(s) participating in the dialogue. The study-reception process is headed by the Standing Commission on Ecumenical Relations, coordinated by the Ecumenical Office (Rev. William A. Norgren, Ecumenical Officer). The Organization of Episcopal Diocesan Ecumenical Officers plays a key role in coordinating local study of the agreement, receiving reports from the local study—which include both evaluation and recommendations for implementation—and reporting back to the Standing Commission, which makes its recommendation to the General Convention, the highest legislative authority. The General Convention may act on the recommendation and establish the degree of acceptance of the document and define implementation. Even before the agreement is formally accepted in this manner, the church at the local and diocesan level is encouraged to take initiatives and modify relationships consistent with acceptable practice on the basis of the agreement.

A one-page preview of the Episcopal Church study of the Lima statement indicates a special character to this study process:

> . . . the Lima Statement was not produced by our church with one other church, but by people from many churches. Breadth of participation is its distinctive feature. This suggests a strategy for study: to repeat the paradigm of the World Council of Churches Faith and Order Commission locally as far as possible. It is highly appropriate to use Lima as an opportunity for getting in touch with as many others as we can in the neighborhood.

The study process, conceived in January and February, 1983, will conclude in February, 1985, with the Standing Commission's recommendation for the General Convention. This recommendation will address not only the issue of formal acceptance of the document but also a process for implementation designed to build consensus and acceptance in the local church. Following the action of the General Convention, a consultation process with other Anglican churches will continue. Eventually, the Anglicans will respond to BEM as a body through the 1988 Lambeth Conference.

The Moravian Church. The Moravian Church is noncredal and cannot deal rigorously with the doctrinal issues of BEM. Biblical witness and fellowship are most important. BEM reception will affect ecumenical relationships and can emerge within the church through the development of worship material. BEM challenges Moravians to reevaluate some traditional practices of worship and polity which have defined their ecclesial identity. The Provincial Elders' Conference is commending BEM for study on the local, regional, and provincial levels by seminaries, task forces, bishops, and congregations. The Southern Provincial Synod will then consider the document in the spring of 1986; the Northern Provincial Synod, in the summer of 1986. The document will be commended for final consideration by the Unity Synod (worldwide Moravian Church) in 1987.

The Lutherans. Generally the Lutherans understand the reception of BEM as the gradual process, distinct from the official response, whereby an ecumenical convergence statement enters the life of the church at its deepest levels, being digested into the life and liturgy of the community. BEM, especially the ministry section, is particularly pertinent for the progress toward the "new" Lutheran Church to be born in 1987.

The American Lutheran Church. The Lima document was first studied by a small group of bishops and pastors. Three seminaries were asked to study the document and over 5,000 churches were invited to purchase reprints[3] of BEM

---

[3]*Baptism, Eucharist, and Ministry*, Special U.S. Lutheran reprint edition. Available from

and submit answers to the four questions posed by Faith and Order. A draft response will first be considered by the Church Council in the spring of 1984, and finally by the Convention later in the year. Responsibility for the reception process has been retained by the General President, Dr. David W. Preus, assisted by Morris A. Sorenson, Jr., Executive Assistant to the President, and Dr. Walter Wietzke, Director of the Division for Theological Education and Ministry.

The Association of Evangelical Lutheran Churches. All the congregations are asked to study the BEM document along with a specially prepared study guide. The congregational response to the four questions will contribute to the Faith and Order response to be passed by the 1984 Convocation.

The Lutheran Church in America. The reception process is being steered by a committee of four persons (Dr. William G. Rusch, staff). According to a long-standing reception process, 300 congregations are randomly selected to study the document and submit their findings. Theologians on seminary faculties with some students, all pastors, and staff persons of the churchwide agencies are encouraged to participate in the study. The Conference of Synodical Bishops will produce an L.C.A. response which must then be passed by the Convention, the highest authority, meeting in July, 1984.

Lutheran Church-Missouri Synod. (Although not represented at the October conference, the LC-MS did provide the following information.) The seminary faculties are currently studying BEM. Their conclusions will provide the basis for a report by the Commission on Theology and Church Relations that will be submitted to the president and chief ecumenical officer of the communion, Dr. Ralph A. Bohlmann, to be forwarded to Geneva as the LC-MS response. This report will be included in the report of the Commission on Theology and Church Relations to the 1986 Convention.

The Presbyterian Church (U.S.A.). The reception of the BEM statement for the Presbyterian Church (U.S.A.) includes the study process leading to the official response for the W.C.C. Faith and Order Commission through the General Assembly, reflection of the document in new standards for worship and ministry for the reunited church, and eventual acceptance into educational materials and congregational life. The response process has been mandated. The long-term reception process is less clear. The response process is headed by the Advisory Committee on Ecumenical Relations and the Ecumenical Coordinating Team, two bodies working together during this period of restructuring the reunited church. (These committees are staffed by Frederick R. Wilson and Lewis H. Lancaster, and include membership of the co-stated clerks, William P. Thompson and James E. Andrews.) Three select congregations from each synod, some presbyteries, and the seminaries will be studying the document and submitting their written responses before the fall of 1984. Other congregations, presbyteries, and

---

the Association of Evangelical Lutheran Churches, Suite 80LL, 12015 Manchester Rd., St. Louis, MO 63131, for 75¢.

General Assembly councils, boards, and agencies may study the document on their own initiative and submit their findings.

A study guide will be made available soon for the selected and voluntary congregations participating in the study. Congregations will be asked what of baptism, eucharist, and ministry they can affirm as rooted in the faith of the church and the Reformed heritage; what they can do at the congregational level to appropriate BEM; and what the implications of the convergence of the churches in BEM are for relations with other churches locally and globally. Both a meeting of up to seventy-five representatives of study groups, March 9-11, 1984, to sharpen and advance the understandings and suggestions drawn from the study, and a small consultation of women examining BEM from women's perspectives will be funded by a grant from Women's Opportunity Giving, United Presbyterian Women. A writing team will draft a Presbyterian Church (U.S.A.) response on the basis of the reports of all parts of the study, to be submitted for action to the General Assembly in 1985 and forwarded to the W.C.C. Faith and Order Commission by December, 1985.

The Reformed Church in America. The R.C.A. will make its initial response to the W.C.C. Faith and Order Commission through the General Synod. The long-term process of reception would mean acceptance by the congregations and using it in worship. It is hoped that this can be accomplished with a strong educational impact through informal discussion groups throughout the church. The possibility of formally incorporating BEM into liturgical practice is opened up by the fact that the Commissions on Theology and Worship are now partici-pating in the study for the R.C.A. official response. The response process is headed by an ad hoc committee of the Commission on Christian Unity (chair: Dr. Charles Wissink; staff: the Rev. Nancy Phillips). Groups of local pastors are participating in the study along with the Commissions on Theology and Worship. The ad hoc committee will draft the response to be submitted to the 1984 General Synod for approval.

The United Church of Christ. The polity of the U.C.C. is multicameral with covenanted plural autonomies. This means that no part of the church's structure can bind any other part except by the intrinsic merit of an action which finds concurrence beyond the originating body. Practically, this requires that the BEM document be studied and responded to throughout the church and that the official response be regarded as that of the General Synod or Executive Council acting as the General Synod *ad interim*. This action does not effect the reception for the whole church. Conferences, Associations, and local churches will receive the document only as they elect to do so by the action of their local constituen-cies. The new book of worship which is being developed reflects the impact of BEM. A study process managed by the Office of the President and involving every level of the church has been approved by both the Council for Ecumenism and the Executive Council. Guidelines were produced to assist the study and response process. Insights resulting from the study are encouraged to be incorporated into the life of the U.C.C. Those studying the document are encouraged to do so ecumenically, since the statement has been produced ecumenically. Selected to participate in the study were two seminaries, two agencies, six theologians, six of the thirty-nine Conferences, and several Associations and congregations. The contact person for the study and the writer of the first draft of the response is the Rev. Thomas E. Dipko. The study process was designed to conclude by the end of 1984, with the official response voted by the Executive Council acting as the General Synod *ad interim*. With the suggested time frame extended to the end of 1985, presumably the General Synod will be able to act on the matter at its next session, in June, 1985.

Friends-Quakers. In spite of being represented in the process that produced the Lima document, BEM does not recognize the Quaker tradition. Quakers have no outward sacraments: no ordination, no eucharist, no baptism. Quakers emphasize the spiritual presence of Christ, the baptism of the Holy Spirit. The liturgical implications of BEM are inappropriate both to the unprogrammed worship of a vocal ministry arising from the silence of the body of the congregation under the inspiration of the living Christ as the Presence "in their midst," and to the programmed, low-Protestant worship pattern of some pastored local meetings. Quakers feel BEM silence with regard to their tradition is a de facto assertion that Quakers are not a Christian church. They would have appreciated some acknowledgment, at least in the form of a footnote, to the Christianity of their witness. As a result, the immediate Quaker "response" to BEM is the feeling of being totally excluded.

Friends General Conference. Any action to respond officially to BEM will be initiated by the Christian Interfaith Relations Committee (Paul Kriese, Clerk). The F.G.C. is an association of *"autocephalous"* churches, called "yearly meetings." Each yearly meeting writes its own statement of faith and discipline and is the last court of appeals. Any changes which would substantially affect matters of faith or practice must have the general approval of the constituent yearly meetings as well as the F.G.C. Central Committee. BEM reception will essentially be an informational process.

Friends United Meeting. The Friends United Meeting will respond officially to BEM. The response process is in the form of continuing discussion on the seminary level and in constituent bodies. The Lima document contributes to the internal discussion of the sacramental nature of Quaker worship and questions of authority and accountability.

The International Evangelical Church. This is a young communion of Pentecostal churches whose theology is yet unwritten. Consequently, there is no place or policy for documents such as BEM. The Lima document could be helpful at this developmental stage in the church's life in the effort to clarify issues of theological practice regarding baptism, eucharist, and ministry. Any reception of

BEM would be entirely in the hands of the governing body of each local church. Should the bishops recommend it to the local pastors, the local churches would be responsible for reception. The College of Bishops have read the BEM document and are distributing it to the pastors of the local churches. It is up to the pastor to take the initiative to offer it to the congregation. Pastors can incorporate BEM into the educational and pastoral ministries and can consult the Lima Liturgy for developing liturgical practices. BEM will be made available to ministry interns in the ministry-training programs.

The Universal Fellowship of Metropolitan Community Churches. A relatively young church with a congregational polity, the U.F.M.C.C. practices the acceptance of baptism, admission to the eucharist, and the acceptance of ordination from other communions. Plans for a reception process include grassroots discussion for reporting to the 1985 General Conference, which may adopt the document. The BEM statement can emerge as a major educational worship text for the communion.

The Christian Church (Disciples of Christ). For Disciples, reception of BEM means claiming it as a pastoral and teaching document. Affirmation by the General Assembly must be followed by the claiming of BEM by the regions and congregations. Long-term reception might mean implementation in the ethical, spiritual, worship, theological, and educational aspects of the church's life.[4] The Council on Christian Unity (Paul A. Crow, President) is in charge of the process for responding to the W.C.C. The Commission on Theology and Christian Unity is engaged in an ecclesiological study of BEM on the national, regional, and local levels. The document is being studied by the seminaries and by national staff; by ecumenical, educational, and ministry commissions on the regional level; and by 300 congregations. Ecumenical study of the document is recommended for the congregations. A report and recommendations from this study will be made by the Commission on Theology and Christian Unity to the Board of Directors of the Council on Christian Unity (the first step of ecumenical policy-making), which will in turn submit its recommendations to the two plenary bodies, the General Board (annual) and the General Assembly (biennial).

The Church of God (Anderson, Indiana). The Church of God is a free church without creed or sacraments. There is no ecclesiastical structure which can formally receive the BEM document. Although there is no "approving" body, study and utilization of the statement can be encouraged. BEM has been presented to the Commission on Christian Unity and to the Division of Church Service. Three persons are to prepare responses. The Commission will decide how to use these in promoting wider study. Plans include articles for publication and utilization in the seminary.

---

[4]A special issue of *Mid-stream, An Ecumenical Journal* will report on BEM implications for Disciples, in July, 1984 (vol. 23, no. 3).

The Church of the Brethren. The Church of the Brethren is a noncredal church in the free-church tradition. Normative statements of belief are applicable to a particular time and are subject to change. The Brethren are among those who feel that the BEM document in certain places excludes their self-understanding and so is seriously flawed. They do, however, accept the opportunity of the convergence statement to reexamine their own tradition. Brethren hopes for BEM are evident in an ecumenical declaration of the Annual Conference in 1982 stating: "Therefore the Church of the Brethren will . . . continue to work for a full and complete mutual recognition of members and ministers of all families within the larger Christian family, and encourage church families to acknowledge fully one another's baptism and observance of the eucharist."[5] The Committee on Interchurch Relations (Robert W. Neff, Executive) has been charged with providing the strategy for implementing the declaration in a reception process for BEM. The reception process is in its initial educational stage of publicizing the Lima document through church publications. The process further includes responses to the document by designated persons, group study by denominational and middle-judicatory staff, receiving dialogue with individuals and congregations, and presenting a response position to the Annual Conference for approval.

The Mennonite Church, The General Conference. The reception of BEM would mean its becoming part of the practice of the local congregations. In this regard Mennonites feel close to the other free churches, the Brethren and Friends. Mennonites were not represented in the process which produced the Lima document. Whereas some of the questions raised by BEM are relevant to Mennonite concerns, other areas are problematic or simply outside their experience. In considering the acceptance of statements, Mennonites regard as important both biblical witness and the presence of the Spirit. Reception inevitably requires a long process concentrated at the local-church level.

The American Baptist Churches in the U.S.A. The American Baptists see their relationship to BEM reception as similar to that of the Brethren and the Mennonites. They have a similar congregation-centered polity which demands reception in practice by the local churches. Also, the various elements of BEM relate unevenly to their practice and experience. The Commission on Christian Unity is in charge of the reception process. Through its network it is making the BEM document available to pastors at cost for study and feedback. Also studying the document are seminary faculty and the regional executive ministers who, as a group, are to respond to the statement and recommend action. Eventually, a response to BEM will be made by the General Board, a representative body without binding legislative authority.

---

[5]Quoted by Robert W. Neff, General Secretary of the Church of the Brethren, in his letter of May 18, 1983, to the Commission on Faith and Order, N.C.C.C.

The Southern Baptist Convention. Given the congregational polity of S.B.C., any type of reception would ultimately have to be done individually by the 36,000 local churches. Decisions made at associational, state, and national levels of the S.B.C. have no binding power over the churches. Moreover, there is no standing committee or agency which is charged with theological statements for the denomination. Thus, there is no process of reception for documents generated outside the denomination. Although a formal reception or response process for BEM is not under consideration, S.B.C. study of the document can be encouraged at the seminary-faculty level and in ecumenical and interdenominational groups.

Looking Ahead

Plenaries on the second and third days of the conference offered the reception teams the opportunity to comment on the perspectives and helpful ideas they had learned from one another, as well as to share the recommendations they would be taking back to their churches as a result of this conference. Several teams commented on the feeling, of exclusion expressed by the free churches, most clearly by the Friends. It was felt important that the episcopal and mainline churches hear what the free churches are saying and be sensitive to the free-church understanding of sacrament. The Christian experience of these churches is important and deserves attention. Several teams from episcopal churches expressed a desire to dialogue with the free churches on the relationship of sacramental life and the life of faith. It was observed that other groups also suffer from marginalization, such as Blacks, women, and Hispanics, and that this is deserving of attention in the consideration of BEM reception. Regrettably, black churches were not well represented at the conference.

The most enthusiastically received "new" idea was that the Lima statement, a document written ecumenically, should be studied ecumenically. This was already part of the study process for a few of the churches but was now being echoed by all. Recommendations were heard that ecumenical study should be introduced at every level of the study and reception process. The exchange of study guides would be helpful to local ecumenical study of BEM. The Association of Evangelical Lutheran Churches offered their publication. Other churches preparing study guides or seriously considering doing so include the Lutheran Church in America, the United Church of Christ, the Episcopal Church, the Reformed Church in America, the Presbyterian Church (U.S.A.), the Roman Catholic Church, and the Orthodox Church in America. Another suggestion to promote ecumenical study was that local councils of churches be encouraged to study the document and that reports from these studies be incorporated into the churches' response process. (It was reported that the study of BEM has already had a renewing effect in the lives of some local and state councils.) A suggestion was heard that local ecumenical study days could be instituted. Another was that ecumenical celebrations of the Lima Liturgy could be held locally on certain occasions, such as during the Week of Prayer for Christian Unity.

The majority of the recommendations shared concerned the desire to expand the study processes of BEM in the churches to involve more persons and groups on all levels, and to begin using it. The wider circulation of the Lima statement to those presently untouched by it, now made more possible by the popularly priced Lutheran reprint edition, was urged. Some will go back to their churches with plans to publicize BEM in church publications, while others will ask for the appropriation of more resources and staff for BEM reception.

Various suggestions were heard as to appropriate ways BEM could be used in the development of denominational educational materials. For pastors, retreats focused on BEM were proposed, and the need for sermon-preparation material based on BEM was expressed. Regarding worship, a recommendation was made that a denominational worship commission develop new liturgical resources based on the Lima statement, as is being done by the U.C.C. and others. The dissemination of worship materials from other traditions was proposed as helpful. A number of ideas were put forward as to how the theological seminaries could be further involved in the BEM reception processes. Suggestions included instituting new courses or seminars on BEM, perhaps ecumenically taught, or simply incorporating the Lima statement in present course work. A recommendation was made to encourage seminary participation in congregations' study of the document; another was to have the seminaries utilize BEM-based liturgies in their daily worship.

The final suggestion shared is that there be a follow-up conference when the responses of the churches are already taking shape, perhaps at the end of 1984, to compare notes and reexamine the implications of receiving the BEM statement into the lives of the churches.

RECEPTION IN HISTORY:
AN ECCLESIOLOGICAL PHENOMENON
AND ITS SIGNIFICANCE

Edward J. Kilmartin

The Faith and Order Commission of the World Council of Churches has communicated the Lima text to the member churches with the request for their reactions.[1] It is hoped that the official responses will contribute to greater clarity in the understanding of these structures of the church, a more profound agreement between the churches on their meaning, and a pastoral practice which, despite all variations among the churches, faithfully reflects a common understanding of the one heritage. The great expectation does not stop here. It also includes the hope that this reception of the common heritage will contribute to a deepening of the awareness of the unity which already exists among the churches and so promote the realization of a visible communion at all levels of ecclesiastical life.[2]

The Faith and Order Commission is confident that the Lima text represents essential aspects of the common tradition of baptism, eucharist, and ministry, but it submits the text to the judgment of the churches. In the process of reception, it is expected that the churches not only will evaluate the material in the light of their current understanding of these institutions but also will exercise self-criticism which is conditioned, above all, by the awareness of the limitations of their traditional understanding and practice of these aspects of the life of faith. It is presupposed that the responses made by official representatives of the churches will include the input of other members at all levels and, as far as possible, the results of dialogue with representatives of other traditions.[3]

---

[1]*Baptism, Eucharist, and Ministry.* Faith and Order Paper 111 (Geneva: World Council of Churches, 1982).

[2]Ibid., pp. vii-x.

[3]Commentaries on Faith and Order's understanding of the reception process are plentiful. Cf. Anton Houtepen, "Reception, Tradition, Communion," in Max Thurian, ed., *Ecumenical Perspectives on Baptism, Eucharist, and Ministry.* Faith and Order Paper 116 (Geneva: W.C.C., 1982), pp. 141-144; William H. Lazareth, *Growing Together in Baptism, Eucharist, and Ministry: A Study Guide.* Faith and Order Paper 114 (Geneva: W.C.C., 1982), pp. 4-8, as well as the whole text which is aimed at fostering the process of reception; and William G. Rusch, "'Baptism, Eucharist, and Ministry'—and Reception," *Dialog* 22

Edward J. Kilmartin (Roman Catholic), S.J., is now Professor of Liturgy at the Pontifical Oriental Institute in Rome, prior to which he was Professor of Liturgy at the University of Notre Dame (1975-83) and Professor of Theology at the Weston College School of Theology (1958-75). He holds an M.A. from Boston College, an M.S. from Holy Cross College, an S.T.L. from Weston College, and an S.T.D. from the Gregorian University in Rome. His most recent book is *Church, Eucharist and Priesthood* (Paulist, 1981), and his articles have appeared in numerous scholarly journals.

There are a variety of modes of communication and structures of communion in the various churches. Hence, it is an open question how the reception process will work out, not only within the individual churches but also in the communication among churches.[4] It is not my intention to attempt to predict how this extremely complicated process might be carried through. In all likelihood it would prove to be an exercise in futility since the Spirit finds ways of bridging human obstacles at the acceptable time. The task of evaluating the model of the common heritage provided by the Lima text also goes beyond the scope of this contribution to the Hyde Park conference.

I have been asked to reflect on the process of reception as an ecclesiological reality and to discuss how it has occurred in history. What we know about the history of the reception process within individual churches and within the communion of churches can alert us to significant factors which make possible effective communication of the life of faith between separated ecclesiastical bodies. This knowledge of the laws which govern ecclesiastical communication— and which are not very different from those that determine the communication of all truly human goods—may contribute to a more realistic approach to the number-one problem of the ecumenical movement: the reception by the churches of one another.

At the outset some observations are made on the concept of reception as a human phenomenon, with special emphasis on reception by a social group and its application to the church. This is followed by examples of reception, drawn mainly from instances which have taken place within one communion of churches. Even though these examples do not immediately relate to the situation of the separated churches, they bring to light certain basic elements and models of the reception process which are applicable to the ecumenical context.

Models of reception based on the understanding and practice of the first millennium are highlighted, for they are a tributary of the dominant ecclesiology of that age: a communion ecclesiology, to which corresponds the reception process envisioned by Faith and Order. Later models, which derive from the late-medieval Western concept of the church as a universal corporation, are not adequate to the task of explaining the process and significance of reception as an ecclesiological reality.[5] The same holds true for the nineteenth-century model

---

(1983): 85-93 (included elsewhere in the present collection). Emmanuel Lanne's lecture at the plenary session of Faith and Order, convened at Lima on January 7, 1982, describes what is involved in the reception of the Lima text ("La 'reception,'" *Istina* 27 (1982): 199-213; an abridged English translation is available: "The Problem of Reception by the Churches," *Ecumenism*, no. 70 (June, 1983), pp. 25-31.

[4]A. Houtepen, "Reception, Tradition, Communion," pp. 144-155; Ulrich Kuhn, "Reception—An Imperative and an Opportunity," in M. Thurian, *Ecumenical Perspectives*, pp. 164-171.

[5]In the West, during the late Middle Ages, the church was viewed as a universal corporation in which clergy and laity gave advice to the pope on important issues. The old Roman legal maxim, *Quod omnes tangit, ab omnibus tractari et approbari debet* (Cod. Just. 5,59, 5,2), had a place and was incorporated into the first authentic, unified, exclusive, and

of reception linked to an excessively hierarchical image of church.[6] In both cases reception is reduced to a juridical category. However, life resists theories. What is true of the first millennium also holds for the second. The ecclesiological reality of reception continues to be a fact of life in all churches.

I. The Phenomenon of Reception

The infinitive "to receive" and the substantive "reception" refer to a process by which some material or spiritual good of one party comes into the possession of another. Full reception of a material good includes physical possession and use. In the full reception of a spiritual good the recipient is intrinsically changed and passes from one spiritual condition to another. Reception of a material good can take place in one moment of time; reception of a spiritual good may involve a long, gradual process.

When a spiritual good is received by a social group as such, the complexity and length of the process are increased, especially when it contributes to a significant transformation and does not somehow already exist in the receiving community or exists only at a low level of social consciousness. Here the corporate will must be formed, which is not identical with the sum total of the individual wills involved. The same holds true for the corporate understanding. Personal subjects are enabled to enter into the corporate will and understanding and so to transcend their previous spiritual condition. But, as in the case of different social groups, degrees of reception depend on volition, intelligence, and the conditioning factors of culture, knowledge, language, etc.

Reception as an ecclesiological reality is a particular instance of the general phenomenon of reception of a spiritual good by a social group. It can be described as a process by which one ecclesiastical body adopts as its own a

---

universal collection of church law, approved by Pope Gregory IX's bull of promulgation, "Rex pacificus," September 5, 1234 (Yves Congar sketches the history of the ecclesiastical use of this maxim in "Quod omnes tangit, ab omnibus tractari et approbari debet," *Revue Historique du Droit Français et Étranger* 35 [1958]: 210-259). But, when agreement was reached on matters of doctrine and discipline by legitimate representatives of the lay and clerical states, it was considered to be the expression of the inspiration of the Spirit and the consensus of the faithful. All had the duty to submit to the decision; no other form of reception was considered (Johannes Mühlsteiger, "Rezeption–Inkulturation–Selbsbestimmung," *Zeitschrift für katholische Theologie* 105 [1983]: 268).

[6]Vatican I furnished the model of a purely hierarchical church with a unilateral approach to papal primacy of teaching and jurisdiction, which threatened to place the pope outside and over the church. This left little room for active reception on the part of the rest of the church. Still, the most notable of all official reports set before that council, one by Bishop Vincent Gässer in the name of the Deputation on Faith, insisted that the pope teaching infallibly is not to be separated from "the cooperation and agreement of the Church, at least in the sense that one does not exclude such collaboration and agreement on the part of the Church" (84th Gen. Cong., July 11, 1870; Mansi 52, 1213c). And, more significantly, Vatican II, which situated the teaching of Vatican I within a broader ecclesiological context, shows that Vatican I really initiated a process of reception, yet to be completed (*Lumen gentium*, ch. III, 18 ff.).

spiritual good which originates in another and acknowledges and appropriates it as applicable to its own life of faith. This process may include a formal juridical act of reception on the part of church officials. Correspondingly, there may also be a response on the part of the other members of the community to the authoritative act in which obedience to formal juridical authority has a place, but the spiritual reception by the whole community includes a degree of consent and possibly judgment as to whether what is being received serves the common good.

Reception as an ecclesiological reality implies the formation of a corporate openness which takes place through bearers of reception who may be juridical or nonjuridical authorities. When a significant spiritual good is newly introduced into a global perception of the life of faith and thereby begins to affect the practice of the faith, a new synthesis of understanding and practice of the faith is initiated. Since this threatens the equilibrium of the community's self-understanding, it may cause a serious negative reaction in some quarters. Elsewhere, the good may be immunized by a superficial adaptation. Examples of these alternative reactions can be illustrated from the history of the early general councils of the church or from the way in which Vatican II's teaching has been "received" or "rejected" within segments of the Roman Catholic Church.

Assimilation of a spiritual good into the life of faith generally involves repeated decisions of authority figures and of the whole social group. In each new historical situation this reception process must be repeated if the spiritual good is to remain alive within the community. In this regard the churches can learn much from the work of German legal historians about the phenomenon of reception. Especially during the last century these scholars have formulated a rather satisfactory explanation of the complicated process by which Roman law was received in Germany.[7] This process, which took several centuries, entailed the intellectual rationalization of the whole of public life. It was initiated by professional lawyers of the Roman school who applied their methods to the whole of life. It also involved the efforts of broader social groups to transform the law, as well as the gradual and radical change of attitude of many millions toward the law.

As in the case of the reception of Roman law in Germany, the process of reception of spiritual goods within the church resists exact analysis. While the phenomenon of reception occurs frequently within churches of one communion and between separated churches, a precise description of the reception process has not generally been made. One of the main difficulties is the frequent inability of scholars to demonstrate whether and to what extent the spiritual good being

---

[7]Franz Wieacker, in *Privatrechtsgeschichte der Neuzeit unter besonderer Berüchsichtigung der deutschen Entwicklung*, 2nd ed. (Göttingen: Vandenhoeck & Ruprecht, 1967), provides the most comprehensive discussion of this process. Alois Grillmeier in "Konzil und Rezeption: Methodische Bemerkungen zu einem Thema der *ökumenischen Diskussion der Gegenwart*," *Theologie und Philosophie* 45 (1970): 322-327, calls attention to the significance of this work for the ecumenical dialogue.

received already exists in the receiving community at some level of conscious-ness.[8]

A good deal of first-class research has been done on the history of local and so-called ecumenical councils of the first millennium, but in no case has the process of reception of doctrinal decisions of local or general councils been sub-mitted to an exact analysis.[9] However, three things can be mentioned about these councils which are relevant to our theme. First, when significant spiritual goods are involved, which already exist in a vital way in the original spiritual resources of the receiving community, the process of reception takes place smoothly. Or, second, as in the case of Nicaea I, Chalcedon, and the rest of the so-called ecumenical councils of the first millennium, reception takes place through a more or less complicated process.[10] Third, these cases of reception of conciliar decisions by the church were neither in fact, nor understood by the churches to be, accomplished by a merely juridical act of acceptance by church officials; rather, the juridical act was viewed as initiating a spiritual process of reception by the whole community.[11]

In the ecumenical context it is vitally important that all concerned recog-nize that the reception of a spiritual good involves a spiritual process. This aware-ness substantially increases the chances that the initial acceptance will be carried through to a really deep integration of that good in the life of the receiving church. Here it may be recalled that separated churches frequently show a cer-tain reticence about admitting their spiritual dependence on one another. Conse-quently, the process of mutual reception of spiritual goods from one another can

---

[8]A. Grillmeier's examples of exogenous receptions of decisions of local councils by the communion of churches in the ante-Nicene period are not convincingly demonstrated ("Konzil und Rezeption," pp. 331-337). He himself notes that the question of reception of local synods of all grades has not been submitted to exact analysis and that it is difficult to find examples of strictly exogenous receptions (ibid., p. 335). Y. Congar finds his attempt to apply the notion of exogenous reception to the one communion of churches "too nar-row" ("La 'reception' comme réalité ecclesiologique," *Revue des sciences philosophiques et théologiques* 56 (1972): 370; an abridged version of this article is found in "Reception as an Ecclesiological Reality," in G. Alberigo and A. Weiler, eds., *Election and Consensus in the Church*, Concilium 77 (New York: Herder & Herder, 1972), pp. 43-68 (here, p. 44).

[9]Numerous monographs give a good account of individual councils and impressive sur-veys of the history of councils, but a careful analysis of the factors and phases which led to the recognition of councils as ecumenical is still not available. This observation of Heinrich Bacht still holds true ("Vom Lehramt der Kirche und in der Kirche," *Catholica* 25 [1971]: 159, note 57).

[10]A. Grillmeier, in "The Reception of Chalcedon in the Roman Catholic Church," *Ecu-menical Review* 22 (1970): 383-411, outlines important stages of the reception of Chalce-don in the West; J. Coman does the same for the Byzantine Church in the same issue ("The Doctrinal Definition of the Council of Chalcedon and Its Reception in the Orthodox Church of the East," pp. 363-382), as does M. Ashjian for the Armenian Church ("The Acceptance of the Ecumenical Councils by the Armenian Church, with Special Reference to the Council of Chalcedon," pp. 348-362).

[11]Since the late Middle Ages, the concept of reception has traditionally been treated in Roman Catholic circles at the level of constitutional law. When linked to a sharp distinction between the teaching and the hearing, passive church, the original rich meaning was lost. Some Roman Catholic scholars in the post-Reformation period explicitly narrowed this

remain for a long time at a superficial level. To illustrate this, examples could be mentioned of adaptations of spiritual goods of the Roman Catholic tradition by some Reformation churches which do not yet represent spiritual reception. However, in the interest of brevity one outstanding case on the other side may suffice. Recently, Otto Hermann Pesch has called attention to the strange ways of the Catholic reception of Luther. After 400 years of polemics, an objective climate has been created by some scholars which makes it possible to speak about Luther in a more positive way and so to evaluate his real significance. At present we are witnessing a certain reception of Luther among Catholic scholars, but, according to Pesch, this is proceeding at a slow pace: Luther is still often misunderstood, immunized, or mistrusted.[12]

Before concluding these observations on reception as an ecclesiological reality, a brief reference to nonreception as an ecclesiological reality is needed to complete the picture. Frequently, discussions of the theme of reception provide only passing reference to this phenomenon, but, as the subsequent analysis of examples of the spiritual communication between churches shows, nonreception of spiritual goods is not a marginal aspect in the history of the church, even within the one communion of churches.

In the patristic age it was generally assumed that complete uniformity of lifestyle in all churches was not necessarily the greater good. Within the one communion of churches there are many cases of refusal to acknowledge that a spiritual good of another church is applicable to one's own life of faith. This caused no undue tension when the good was recognized as appropriate to the life of the other church, and the other could agree that the nonreception in no way touched the profound communion which existed between the two ecclesiastical bodies. It could also happen that juridically valid decisions of church officials were not accepted by the other members of a church because they were not considered to serve the common good. The example of refusal to accept a validly elected official comes to mind. History shows that initial nonacceptance of juridically valid decisions of church officials does not necessarily signal the end of the reception process. It may only indicate that the decision is not oppor-

---

concept to an act of religious obedience (Y. Congar, "La 'reception,' " p. 391; Eng. trans., p. 60; H. Müller, Der Anteil der Laien an der Bischofswahl. Kanonistische Studien und Texte 29 [Amsterdam: B. R. Grüner, 1977], p. 217). In recent years Reformation and Roman Catholic scholars have tended to agree that reception must be understood as spiritually extending official decisions into the life of the church and so contributing to their effectiveness (Y. Congar, "La 'reception,' " pp. 391-401; Eng. trans., pp. 60-68; H. Müller provides a review of literature on this subject (in Der Anteil, pp. 213-220).

    [12]" 'Ketzerfürst' und 'Vater im Glauben,' " in Hans Friedrich Geiser et al., Weder Ketzer noch Heiliger. Luthers Bedeutung für den ökumenischen Dialog (Regensburg: Pustet, 1982), pp. 123-174. Pesch asks how reception of Luther should take place. According to him, prescinding from the fact that in Catholic theology Luther's ideas already have a foothold, though he may not be consciously recognized as father of these goods, Lutheran teaching in the field of word and sacrament, faith and works, the relation of the papacy to the church, etc., should be carried further through ecumenical dialogue involving Catholics and Lutherans.

tune, that it does not really touch the life of the community.[13] It does not necessarily even signify an act of disobedience to formal authority.[14] In this connection one can cite the bull "Execrabilis" of Pius II (January 18, 1460), which
forbade the appeal to a council over the pope.[15] It was received in the Roman
Catholic Church only after protracted discussion in which Pius II had to inter-
vene to discourage the reception of his own conciliarist position espoused before
his ordination to the priesthood. Vigorous opposition may actually be a sign of
the beginning of a process of reception through which a decision eventually finds
a place in the life of the church. In doctrinal matters the Council of Nicaea I
(325) provides a prime example of this.

II. Examples of Reception/Nonreception as an Ecclesiastical Reality

The foregoing description of reception/nonreception as an ecclesiological
reality, based on the history of the phenomenon of reception in the church,
includes some concrete examples. In this section a more detailed analysis of
instances is undertaken. In the past few centuries liturgical scholars have provided impressive scholarly research on various aspects of the process of reception
of liturgical goods. Less attention has been paid to the reception of law and
custom. In the area of the history of councils, recent publications have dealt
with the process of reception of local and ecumenical councils of the first millennium, as well as with the councils' self-understanding of their authority and the
value of reception of their resolutions by the whole church.

A. Reception of Liturgical Practices

I begin with reception and nonreception of liturgical practices of one church
by another, possibilities implied in the Lima text. In the interest of brevity,
observations on reception are confined to some general remarks regarding positive results. Special emphasis is placed on the negative aspects of some outstanding examples of reception, because they seem to bring out important aspects of
what is involved in a reception which proves beneficial for a church.

There was a rich exchange of liturgical practices in the early church during
the formation of the great liturgical traditions of the East and West. It was conditioned by the conviction that all churches hold the same faith and so have

---

[13]Decisions of church officials are opportune when they correspond to an experience
which impregnates and structures the existence of believers. E.g., in the matter of teaching
the faith, the corresponding experience in the lives of believers determines the ease with
which a doctrine is received and the interest which it evokes (G. Widmer, "Sens ou non-sens
des énoncés théologiques," *Revue des sciences philosophiques et théologiques* 51 [1967]:
650).

[14]H. Bacht observes that nonreception in itself does not constitute an act of formal
disobedience. It only means that the decision is lifeless, so it does not contribute to edifica-
tion here and now ("Vom Lehramt," p. 161).

[15]Denziger-Schönmetzger 1375.

their measure of gifts to share with one another. The openness of the churches to each other made the reception process normal, and this exchange was mutually beneficial.

The received liturgical practices were integrated into communities of different cultures, with diversities of genius and conditions of life. These different historical situations influenced diverse spiritual experiences of the one faith and so had a direct influence on the interpretation given to the received practices. However, the introduction of foreign liturgical practices could and did lead to a new understanding of the liturgy and set in motion profound changes in the spiritual experience of the faith. In this regard an interesting example is furnished by the widespread fourth-century reception of the Spirit *epiclesis* in the Divine Liturgy of the East, under the influence of controversies over the divinity of the Holy Spirit and presumably by the liturgical *epiclesis* of the *Apostolic Tradition* of Hippolytus. This had a direct bearing on the development of the peculiar Eastern theology of the Lord's Supper.

Prescinding from the question of the enduring value of the traditional Orthodox theology of the Lord's Supper,[16] it can confidently be stated that not all instances of reception of liturgical practices have been good for a church. If we confine ourselves to instances of reception of liturgical goods within the sphere of the Western church, some significant examples can be described as mixed blessings with unforeseen but clearly negative results.

The Romanization of Eastern liturgies, after certain Eastern churches reestablished communion with Rome, can be mentioned. As a result of a long, uninterrupted policy of imposing Roman practices, initiated by Rome or missionaries, Catholic kings or local hierarchy, these Eastern churches were brainwashed to such a degree that they tended to look on Roman discipline as more authentic than their own venerable tradition. Moreover, the integration of Roman liturgical practices, though not always without value, had the effect of obscuring the clear structure of the original liturgies in many cases. In the end, the process of reception was not carried through to inculturation and so was doomed to failure.

A different result obtained in the case where Pope Gregory VII (1073-1085), for reasons which he considered serious, forced the substitution of the Roman liturgy for the ancient Spanish liturgy.[17] Initially, one could not speak of the reception of the Roman liturgy in Spain. Still, the liturgical variants of the Roman tradition were not so great as to be an obstacle to full reception. Gregory VII decided against the ancient Spanish liturgy because he was convinced that it was tainted with the heresy of adoptionism. In this respect his action

---

[16]The stress on the pneumatological side of the eucharistic celebration in traditional theology of the Byzantine Church causes uneasiness within the Western tradition. Here is emphasized the christological aspect which is objectively more in harmony with the ante-Nicene understanding that Christ is host of the meal, the dispenser and food of eternal life.

[17]Juan F. Riviera, "Mosarabic Liturgy," in J. Vellian, ed., *The Romanizing Tendency.* Syrian Church Series 8 (Kottayam, India: K. P. Press, 1975), pp. 46-53; and his "Gregorio VII y la Liturgia Mozarabic," *Revista Espanola de Teologia* 2 (1942): 3-33.

did not conflict with the tolerant attitude concerning diversity of liturgical practices which seemed to have prevailed during most of the first millennium. In
this period one church generally accepted practices of another as legitimate even
where it was convinced that its own usages were more conformed to Scripture
and the whole tradition, as long as the alien practices did not seem to endanger
the essentials of the life of faith.

Pope Gregory the Great (590-604) formulated a basic principle for judging
the value of diversity of liturgical practices. Although the triple immersion was
almost universally observed in the rite of baptism throughout the West, in the
context of the Spanish church he found no difficulty in approving a single immersion.[18] The Archbishop of Seville, Leander (d. 600), asked Gregory whether
the custom could be retained in order not to support the Arian interpretation
that the triple immersion symbolized the three distinct natures in the Trinity.
Gregory responded that the practice seemed reasonable to him and added: "In
the matter of preservation of the one faith a differentiated custom of the Holy
Church causes no damage."[19]

Ambrose of Milan provides a classic example of the local church's self-understanding of its freedom in the matter of determination of liturgical practices.
He accepted in principle the rule that Rome should be followed. However, the
Church of Milan practiced footwashing after the water bath in the baptismal rite,
while Rome did not. On this subject he wrote: "In all matters I desire to follow
the Roman Church. However, we possess the capability of judgment proper to
man. Consequently if what is done elsewhere corresponds more to reason, we
more correctly hold to that practice."[20]

We have seen that acceptance of liturgical practices of another church can
result in negative effects if not carried through to inculturation. This model of
reception of Roman practices by Eastern churches, which has a place between
full reception and nonreception, is exemplified by two classic examples drawn
from the early Middle Ages: the acceptance of the Roman liturgy in Germany
and the Mainz Pontifical by Rome.

The adoption of the Roman liturgy in Germany came in the wake of the
evangelization of that territory by Roman missionaries, beginning in the sixth
century. As Germany came under the influence of Rome, the educated people
adopted the Roman culture, in good measure. This included the Latin language,

---

[18]Ep. 1, 43 (CCSL 140, 48; PL 77, 497). Gregory the Great maintained the threefold
immersion for Rome, but, in general, he accepted the practice of one immersion as a legitimate option. He reasoned that the first form symbolizes the three days' rest of Christ in
the grave and venerates the Trinity; the second symbolizes the unity of the Trinity. Hence,
the traditional use has a purely symbolic value. See Ep. 1, 43 (CCSL 140, 48-49; PL 77,
497C-497A).

[19]It is noteworthy that the fifteenth canon of the Canons of the Holy Apostles, established as eighty-five in the East around 550, prohibits the use of a single immersion. It reads
in part: "If any bishop or presbyter does not perform the one initiation with three immer-
sions, but by one immersion only . . . let him be deposed."

[20]De sacramentis III, 1, 5 (CSEL 73, 40).

which also became the language of the liturgy. While the Roman liturgy, when taken over by Germany, underwent many changes as the traits of the local culture were added to it, the Latin language was retained. As a result, the vast majority of the people—who could not understand Latin—simply became bystanders. This probably contributed, in greater measure than the influence of newer theological developments that tended to foster a clericalized liturgy, to the eventual removal of the laity from active participation in the public worship of the church.[21]

The reception of the Mainz Pontifical by Rome in the tenth century, and afterward by the whole Western church, included the acceptance of a culturally conditioned usage, which remained a foreign body until a theological interpretation was provided, and which had grave consequences. The practice of handing over the liturgical instruments for the eucharist in the ordination of presbyter—the paten and cup—was introduced in Germany and transmitted to Rome through the Mainz Pontifical. This gesture corresponds to the secular ritual investment of officials through the bestowal of symbols of their offices.

In the new climate this rite upset the clear lines of the ordination ceremony which had as the high point the long prayer of ordination and the imposition of hands by the bishop. Attention was shifted away from the ecclesiological significance of the episcopal gesture which symbolized the new relation of the ordinand to the bishop and so to the church. The way was open to a new theology of priesthood based on the liturgy itself. By the thirteenth century the new rite of *traditio instrumentorum*, with the accompanying words, "Receive the power of offering sacrifice in the church for the living and dead . . . ," was understood more commonly to be the very kernel of the presbyterial ordination.[22] This furnished support for the opinion that ordination confers a personal power, enabling the candidate to consecrate bread and wine even outside the context of the ecclesial celebration of the eucharist. This common interpretation of the rite of *traditio instrumentorum* and of the nature of the power bestowed in ordination has undergone a change in this century. While the Roman *magisterium* has definitely opted for the rite of laying on of hands as the kernel of presbyterial ordination,[23] Catholic theology more generally links the power of the ordained to an ecclesial context in a radical way. However, the full implica-

---

[21]Hans B. Meyer, "Zur Frage der Inkulturation der Liturgie," *Zeitschrift für katholische Theologie* 105 (1983): 15-16.

[22]The *Decretum pro Armenis* of the Council of Florence, linked to the bull "Exsultate Deo" (November 22, 1439) which established union between Rome and the Armenian Church, provides instructions concerning the sacraments drawn mainly from Thomas Aquinas, *De articulis fidei et ecclesiae sacramentis*. It affirms that the rite of *traditio instrumentorum* is the essential matter and form of the presbyterial ordination (DS 1326).

[23]Pius XII, in the apostolic constitution "Sacramentum Ordinis," November 30, 1947, affirmed that, whatever may have been the sacramental value of the rite of *traditio instrumentorum* in the past, it no longer is to be considered the essential rite of presbyterial ordination (DS 3857-3859).

tions of the re-reception of the old tradition have not yet been worked out in Catholic theology.

B. Reception of Law and Customs

The whole matter of reception of canons issued in the East and West with a view to providing direction for the moral life and to order church discipline and administration has not been fully and systematically studied for the period of the first millennium. However, one gets the impression that the canons of one church were received by the other only insofar as they were judged to be beneficial.

The Council of Constantinople I (381), eventually recognized as the second ecumenical council, was not immediately received in the West, especially because of the third canon which promoted Constantinople as the "New Rome."[24] Pope Leo the Great received the Council of Chalcedon only in the matter of doctrine.[25] The Council of Constantinople III (680-681), listed as the sixth ecumenical council, ratified the Canons of the Holy Apostles, referring in its second canon to the "so-called of the Apostles," but Pope Leo II approved only the decisions which concerned doctrine.[26] The Synod of Constantinople of 692 is considered by the Greeks to be the continuation of the fifth and sixth ecumenical councils and so is called Quinsext. It issued 102 canons. Pope Sergius (687-701), a Syrian by birth, refused to approve these canons for the West since they had little relevance for this sphere of church life. Canon 3a of the Council of Sardica (343-344), which was intended to be a general council of the church, agrees that problems between churches should be referred to the bishop of Rome, whose decision should be accepted "for the honor of the memory of the blessed apostle Peter."[27] This canon was not received in the East, probably in great part because it did not give sufficient place to the emperor's authority. It is paraphrased, and immunized, in various ways in Eastern *epitomes* of canons.[28]

On the whole, variations in styles of life of individual churches were not considered to be symptomatic of disunity during the early period of the ancient Catholic Church. Toward the end of the first millennium, and afterward, they became a source of mutual criticism. The tolerant attitude toward local customs, characteristic of great church leaders of the ancient Catholic Church, can be exemplified by the advice given a certain Januarius and Augustine of Canterbury,

---

[24]Canon 3 reads: "The bishop of Constantinople is to be honored next after the bishop of Rome" (PL 84, 135 C).

[25]Ep. 141, 1: "in sola causa fidei" (PL 54, 1029A).

[26]Ep. "Regi regum" ad Constantium IV imp., August, 682 (DS 562: "his quae definita sunt ab ea.").

[27]DS 133.

[28]In George Mastrantonis, ed., *Ancient Epitome of the Sacred Canons of the Eastern Orthodox Church* (St. Louis: Ologos, n.d.), the canon reads: "A bishop of the province who is engaged in any litigation should not appeal to outside bishops. But if Rome hears the cause, even outsiders may be present" (p. 34).

both of whom were concerned about pluralism in church customs. The former asked Augustine of Hippo about the meaning of the variety of customs of different regions and churches. What attitude should be adopted toward unfamiliar practices? Augustine found a solution in the saying of Ambrose concerning fasting on the Sabbath: "When I am at Rome, I fast on the Sabbath, when I am here I do not fast."[29]

The problem facing Augustine of Canterbury, sent by Pope Gregory the Great to evangelize the Anglo-Saxons, was much more serious. In the work of establishing the Church of England, the question of fixing a whole range of customs which would govern the life of the church was raised. Augustine sought Gregory's advice: "Since there is one faith, why are the customs of the churches so diverse; and one custom of Masses exists in the Roman Church and another in the churches of Gaul?" Gregory responded:

> Your fraternity knows the custom of the Roman Church in which you recall you were nurtured. But I prefer that either in the Roman Church, or in the churches of Gaul, or in any church, you carefully choose what you have found which can please more the omnipotent God, and that you insert into the Church of England, which is new in the faith . . . those things you are able to gather from many churches. . . . Therefore select from any individual church those things which are pious, religious, correct, and place them . . . in custom among the English.[30]

Augustine, Ambrose, Gregory the Great, and the nobleminded Fathers of the golden age of Greek patristic literature instinctively recognized that a measure of self-determination belongs to Christian communities in the matter of law and customs. Moreover, the practice of the churches demonstrates their self-awareness of this freedom, which is simply one expression of the natural tendency of local churches to clothe the life of faith in forms derived from the surrounding culture.

It is a fact of history that the church can only express its life of faith, in its dimensions, by using a culture. But, since there exists no superior culture which transcends and, at the same time, includes all cultures, the full reception of Christian faith, conveyed in the clothing of one culture to believers of another culture, entails inculturation. The inculturation of the church may be described as

> the integration of the Christian experience of a local church into the culture of its people, in such a way that this experience not only expresses itself in the elements of this culture, but becomes a force that animates, orients and innovates this culture so as to create a

---

[29]Ep. 54 *ad Januarium* I, 1 (CSEL 34, 161; PL 33, 201).
[30]Ep. 11, 64 (PL 77, 1186-1187).

new unity and communion, not only in the culture in question but
also as an enrichment of the Church universal.[31]

Through this process of inculturation the spiritual reception of Christianity by
a specific people is fully realized.

This inculturation first took place when the gospel was planted in the Jew-
ish-Palestinian milieu. Later on the faith was received by the surrounding peoples
and was expressed in the dominant culture of the Mediterranean lands. When the
church had to express its faith in other ways than that of Hellenistic culture,
it could do so only through some specific culture. The new ways of expressing
the faith suited to different cultures are not only desirable. Even more, human
beings are deeply bound to their culture, which is an element of their identities
and personalities. Consequently, inculturation is a basic principle of the life of
faith.

The problem of inculturation has received considerable attention in recent
times as Third World countries emerge from political and cultural dependence
on European masters. One often hears that missionaries took responsibility for
Christianizing Africa or South America, but now Black Africans or South Ameri-
cans must take responsibility for Africanizing or South-Americanizing Christianity. Inculturation involves the incarnation of the one faith, expressed in categories of thought, symbols, liturgical practices, and ethical models which are
newly formulated by a local people with fidelity both to the cultural heritage
and to Christian revelation. This process raises serious problems for Third World
countries in many areas of Christian life. What cultural goods are capable of
being integrated into the life of faith of the local church?[32]

In theory the possibility of inculturation of the Christian faith into Third
World countries causes no difficulties for European churches, but many problems can be envisioned regarding the reception of the product of inculturation.
This will be made easier to the extent that the Third World churches are recognized as truly churches, capable of self-determination in fidelity to the gospel.
As history shows, in the matter of reception and nonreception within the one
communion of churches, all depends on the persuasion that the other church
can bring forth spiritual goods out of its own spiritual resources which foster
its own life and, at times, can be appropriated by other churches for their own
enrichment.[33]

---

[31]Ary R. Crollius, "What Is New about Inculturation? A Concept and Its Implications,"
Gregorianum 59 (1978): 735.

[32]J. Mühlsteiger, in "Rezeption," pp. 276-277, note 69, refers to the tribal norms of the
Sudan which determine the validity and stability of marriage and which make the Christian
marriage ceremony a mere added blessing, as well as to the practice of polygamy which has
an honored place in some black African cultures. H. Meyer in "Zur Frage," pp. 16-23, offers
examples of the possibilities of incorporating certain cultural goods of emerging nations into
the liturgy.

[33]A patristic principle that an individual author's works should be received primarily on
the basis of their spiritual authority corresponds to this outlook. E.g., the *Decretum Gelasia-*

C. Reception of Doctrine

The examples of reception and nonreception of liturgical practices and of law or custom can serve to illustrate a long tradition which supports both the benefits of mutual exchange and diversity of lifestyle within the churches. The history of reception of doctrinal matters shows that a somewhat different approach obtains. During the first millennium the event of conciliar decisions about fundamental doctrines of the church was of interest to all the churches of the one communion. It was vitally important that all churches could agree with the resolutions, not only as far as content but also with the formulations themselves. Consequently, reception often involved a complex process. The possiblity of different formulations of the same dogma within a particular council was not envisioned. This fact makes the decision of the fifteenth-century Council of Florence all the more interesting. I will return to this topic after considering some aspects of the process of reception of doctrine in the ancient Catholic Church.

1. *Doctrinal decisions of local councils.* The reception of the judgment of the Synod of Antioch (268) by the churches of the East and West represents a good example of the authority which a local synod could exercise within the one communion of churches. The Fathers of the synod condemned Paul of Samosata, who was reported to have used the term *"homoousios"* when describing the relation of the Logos to the Father. The Council of Nicaea I, in turn, employed the same term in its confession of faith regarding the relation of Son to Father, but such was the authority of Antioch in the whole church that the adherents of Nicaea found it necessary to defend its presumed condemnation of Paul's use of *"homoousios."* Athanasius, the great preacher of the teaching of Nicaea, appealed to the orthodoxy of the Fathers of the Council of Antioch, proved by the fact that they actually handed on the divine *paradosis.* So it was not the word *"homoousios"* which came to the foreground but the Fathers who handed on the faith. Hence, Athanasius insisted that the word must be interpreted in its historical context.[34] However, he did not think that any other word could suffice in the context of either council. According to him the formulas served as a kind of transparency for the intention of the faith. Whoever accepted the content of the doctrine of a council should also accept the words which expressed it.[35]

num, which derives in part from Pope Gelasius (492-496), refers to writings which are received by the Roman Church for spiritual reading. The main norm is the moral and spiritual authority of the author (*De libris in usum vitae religiosae recipiendis*, DS 353). Some works of Origen are received because of the authority of Jerome (DS 354). The works of heretics or schismatics "The Catholic and Apostolic Roman Church in no way receives" (DS 354).
[34]H. J. Sieben, *Die Konzilsidee der Alten Kirche.* Konzilien-geschichte. Serie B: Untersuchungen (Paderborn: Schöningh, 1979), pp. 50-51.
[35]Letter on the Decrees of Nicaea I: "If anyone makes a serious study, he will recognize that, even if the words are not in the Scriptures, at least the doctrine which they express is really found there" (PG 25, 453).

The factual reception of local councils by the communion of churches in the ante-Nicene period was conditioned by the conviction that each church is truly church and so can speak to the other churches and for the other churches since all live from the same Spirit who guides the decisions.[36] The letter of the Synod of Antioch (268) reads in part: "To Dionysius and Maximus and all those who exercise with us the office in the inhabited earth, to the bishops, priests and deacons and the whole Catholic Church under heaven."[37] The synodal letter of the Council of Arles (314) displays confidence that absent bishops, if present, would agree with its resolutions:

> Since the body of Christ is in each place, although the place in which the assemblies of the members of the whole body . . . can be different. . . . Therefore also you [Pope Sylvester], as present in the Spirit, could speak in unison with us and with a like view could teach concerning these questions which we have discussed and regulated corresponding to ecclesiastical law.[38]

While all churches could speak for the *whole* church, in principle, it is important to note what constituted the authority of conciliar decisions in the ancient Catholic Church. It rested partially on the known orthodoxy of the participants, but, ultimately, the claim to represent the whole communion of churches of the past and present had to be realized by the ability of the council to evoke reception by all the churches.

2. *Doctrinal decisions of ecumenical councils.* What has been said about local councils of the early church holds also for the so-called ecumenical councils. The authority of the councils ultimately rested on the content of the decisions, so the reception process could be protracted. The relationship between reception and the authority of the ecumenical councils of the first millennium has been formulated in various ways by theologians and historians of councils. In the opinion of this writer, the description given by Hermann Josef Sieben is the best to date. In his excellent study of the idea of a universal council in the ancient Catholic Church, Sieben found that a consistent view emerged from Nicaea I to Nicaea II (787). It was determined by the notions of *consensio antiquitatis et universitatis* and the function of the Spirit who grounded the horizontal and vertical consensus. According to Sieben, this view included three decisive theological aspects of the conciliar self-understanding of a universal council. First, the council considered itself to have a high measure of authority and to be mediator of the twofold consensus in the power of the Spirit. Second, this

---

[36]Y. Congar, in "Konzil als Versammlung und grundsätzliche Konziliarität der Kirche," in J. B. Metz and W. Kern, eds., *Gott in Welt* II (Freiburg im Br.: Herder & Herder, 1964), refers to the Council of Arles (314): "praesente Spiritu Sancto et angelis ejus" (p. 149). He also gives a long list of texts which employ Mt. 18:20 to ground the notion of divine support for the councils (pp. 157-165).

[37]A. Grillmeier, "Konzil und Rezeption," p. 333, note 33.

[38]Ibid., p. 334, note 34.

claim of the council brought into prominence the importance of the reception of the decisions of the council by the church universal. Third, the claim also meant that the council was unconditionally bound to the teaching of Scripture and the preaching of it as handed on through the church.[39]

The claim of the council to represent the consensus of the whole church at that moment in history, the so-called horizontal consensus, meant that this had to be secured by reception. The *universitas* had to acknowledge its own truth by reception. From this standpoint, the council was a hazardous project. However, the claim to represent the *consensio antiquitatis* meant that the council had to demonstrate this consensus. Hence, the scope of its possibilities was limited. Only that could be taught which could be demonstrated to correspond to Scripture and the preaching of the economy. Correspondingly, the whole church had the right and duty to test the claim to the so-called vertical consensus. Here, again, the council showed itself to be a hazardous project. In short, in the ancient Catholic Church the problematic of the universal council, under both aspects of consensus, was inseparably linked with the problem of reception. The fact that the success of the council was not automatically guaranteed from the outset points to the awareness of the primacy of the content of the conciliar decisions over whatever formal juridical authority it could claim.

The background and acts of the Council of Toledo XIV (684) provide a good example of the awareness that the vertical consensus—and, so, the content of the resolutions—is the chief criterion for the ecumenicity of a council. Pope Leo II, who understood himself to be the chief preacher of the vertical consensus, asked the Spanish bishops to review the decision of the Council of Constantinople III (681). This council, listed as the sixth ecumenical council, condemned Monotheletism.[40] Leo II, who confirmed the teaching of this council, requested that the Spanish bishops support it with their *auctoritas*.[41] At the Council of Toledo XIV, the bishops of the Carthaginian Church province, together with the representatives of five other Spanish church provinces, tested the claim of Constantinople to vertical consensus and reached a favorable decision.[42] Alternatively, the theologians of Charlemagne tested the claim of the Council of Nicaea II, that its decision regarding the veneration of icons represented the consensus of the past and the present, with different results. In the *Libri Carolini*, authored by them, the teaching of Nicaea II was judged *not* to reflect the "purity of the universal faith and the authority of the whole of the churches."[43]

What is particularly noteworthy about these examples is the presupposition

[39]H. Sieben, *Die Konzilsidee*, pp. 511-516.
[40]DS 550-559.
[41]H. Sieben, *Die Konzilsidee*, p. 340.
[42]The decision of the Council of Toledo XIV reads, in part: "And so the *acta concilii* are venerated by us and stand received insofar as (*in quantum*) they do not disagree with previous councils, indeed, insofar as they seem to agree with them." In other words, the council is received insofar, i. e., because it agrees with previous councils (ibid., p. 341).
[43]*Libri Carolini* IV. 28.

that the vertical consensus, which necessarily includes the element of formal authority, has a position of priority over the horizontal consensus. The vertical consensus is ultimately decisive because the truth of faith is, from its essence, a truth handed on.[44] It is also significant for our theme that the negative reaction of the Frankish theologians to Nicaea II was not simply due to the fact that the faulty Latin translation of the Greek text of the council made it difficult for them to understand the issue at stake. In all truth, the matter did not really touch their lives of faith. When conciliar decisions do not relate directly to the life of faith of a church, one can hardly expect that they will be considered important or even understandable.[45]

3. *A new model of conciliar consensus.* In the ancient Catholic Church there never was a question of posing two formulations of the same dogma and obtaining agreement that either suffices to express the meaning intended by the council. Councils recognized the distance between the aim of the council and the formulations of the doctrine. At the same time, the participants were satisfied that one formula served the intention of the faith of all.[46] This does not mean that factual misunderstandings were excluded. For example, the Roman legates at the Council of Chalcedon did not object to the Niceno-Constantinopolitan Creed which was canonized by the council. Yet the Creed, received by the Council of Constantinople I (381), was formulated in terms of the Cappadocian theology of the procession of the Spirit. The Roman legates understood the Greek *ekporeuomenon*, a term used exclusively for the procession of the Spirit from the Father through the Son, to be equivalent to the Latin *procedere*, which

---

[44]Maximus the Confessor provides a classic formulation of the primacy of the content of conciliar decisions over formal authority. In the *Gesta Bizyae* of August/September 656, he rejected the idea that a council becomes valid by imperial confirmation. It is the content of faith, the "rectitude of dogma," which makes the council valid (PG 90, 145-148). In other words, formal authority stands at the service of the faith, not vice versa.

[45]The Council of Vienna, reckoned in the West as the fifteenth ecumenical council, furnishes an example of a decision which was so historically conditioned and significant only for school theology that it was scarcely understood and had little effect on the church as a whole. Its constitution, "Fidei catholicae," of May 6, 1312, defined that the soul is the *forma corporis humani per se et essentialiter* (DS 902). What this teaching intends is contained in Christian anthropology before and after the council.

[46]However, according to Augustine, the individual's participation in the memory of the church through participation in a conciliar decision involves more than the will to bind oneself to the council and the ability to repeat its teaching verbally. Formulas of councils do not substitute for personal appropriation of the doctrine, formulated in one's own words while conformed to Scripture and the conciliar dogma. In the exchange between Augustine and the Arian Bishop Maximinus, the latter said, "If you ask my faith, I hold that faith which was not only expressed but also confirmed with signatures by 330 bishops of Rimini." Augustine responded: "I already said, and I repeat it, because you refused to answer: State your faith concerning the Father and the Son and the Holy Spirit." And he continued: "You did not tell me your faith, but named the council of Rimini. I want to know your faith. . . . Don't send me to those writings which . . . are not at hand or whose authority I do not hold. Tell me what you believe about the Father and the Son and the Holy Spirit" (*Coll. contra Max.* 2-4 [PL 42, 710-711]; H. Sieben, *Die Konzilsidee*, pp. 88-89).

describes the procession *a Patre Filioque*. Hence, agreement was reached on the basis of terminological ambiguity.[47]

There has never been full agreement between the East and West on the dogmatic formulation of the procession of the Spirit. This was a key issue at the Council of Florence which convened in 1439 to heal the breach between the Latin Church and certain Byzantine churches. This council provides a new model of doctrinal dialogue, for, in this instance, the discussions about the contrasting doctrinal positions of estranged churches produced agreement, however short-lived, on the subject of different formulations of the same dogma: the procession of the Holy Spirit.

Following the explanations of the Latin and Greek approaches to the interpretation of the procession of the Spirit, the Eastern bishops present at the council recognized the *Filioque* as the legitimate expression of the faith of the Latin Church. The same recognition was accorded to the *per Filium* in the context of the Byzantine perception of the faith by the Latin Church. According to the bull "Laetentur coeli," issuing from the sixth session of the council, July 6, 1439, the different formulas signify one and the same faith, and that is why the churches unanimously agreed to union.[48]

The mutual recognition was grounded on the awareness that the formulas were employed by the Eastern and Western Fathers and were consecrated by the ancient traditions of both churches. But this agreement seems to imply, at a deeper level, that one and the same mystery of faith can be expressed differently at the same moment in history without endangering the unity of faith. The Roman Catholic Church has never repudiated this resolution of Florence, which it considers traditionally to be the seventeenth ecumenical council. But, can this approach of the council be justified theologically? Georges Dejaifve has studied this question in connection with the teaching of Vatican II's Decree on Ecumenism, which addresses the question of pluralism in the various expressions of the Christian life of faith.[49] From the relevant passages of the decree,[50] he concluded that it is open to the possibility of pluralism in the formulation of the same dogma.

At the risk of oversimplifying this delicate problem, the theological justification for the presupposition objectively underlying the decision of Florence can be outlined in three steps. First, the object of the act of faith is Christ and his saving mysteries mediated after the resurrection of Christ through the personal witness of faith, beginning with the personal testimony of the apostles. They witnessed to it by their preaching, their example, and the institutions which they created under the inspiration of the Spirit. So it is by the witness of human

---

[47]J. M. Garrigues, "La procession du Saint-Esprit dans la tradition latine du premiers millénaire," *Contacts* 73 (1971-1973): 302-303.

[48]Mansi 31, 1030.

[49]"Diversité dogmatique et unité de la Revelation," in *Una Sancta et Confessiones chrétiennes*. Series oecumenica (Rome: Pontifical Oriental Institute, 1977), pp. 195-204.

[50]*Decree on Ecumenism*, nos. 4.7, 14.3, 17-18.

beings that God the Father reveals self in Christ through the Spirit. Consequently, at the level of expression, revelation shows the traits proper to the subject who transmits it. Second, on the side of the witnesses of revelation there intervenes legitimate diversity in perception and expression of the mystery being communicated. The original diversity, exemplified in the Gospels "according to" the four evangelists, continued after the apostolic age. The one faith was received in different ways in different places, corresponding to the genius and conditions of life of peoples. Third, a peculiar genius conditions a diverse spiritual experience of the event of revelation and has a direct bearing on its comprehension and dogmatic formulation. Formulations of revelation are a tributary of the concrete experience of faith lived by a community, whether this be in the form of dogmas or liturgy which crystallizes the governing interests of churches.

From these considerations it can safely be stated that diversity of dogmatic formulations does not necessarily prejudice the unity of faith, for they can represent the same mystery from different perspectives which are neither superimposable nor mutually exclusive. This seems to be the lesson we can draw from the model of the Council of Florence, where agreement on the intention of faith and sufficient reflection of the apostolic teaching decided the issue, at least at the moment of the council.

Applying this viewpoint to the ecumenical dialogue between the churches, it seems correct to say that the various churches should retain their right, in principle, to formulate their own understanding of the faith based on fidelity to the divine *paradosis*. Other churches should be prepared to recognize these formulations without prejudice to the principle that all attempts to formulate the faith are not necessarily legitimate. To assure orthodoxy all confessions should confront together the authority of the apostolic faith and verify together the aptitude of their dogmatic formulation to express correctly the common heritage. Among the basic criteria for recognition of another church's teaching can be listed two rules: (1) Diverse formulations of the same dogma which are mutually exclusive cannot be admitted in common. (2) Formulas can be complementary when originating from different global perceptions of the life of faith.

All churches should reckon with the limited aspects of their dogmatic statements and assume the possibility of different formulations of the same dogma. To the extent that one can accept this principle, and so the relativity of all dogmatic statements and their binding to concrete historical situations of churches, another principle follows regarding the common formulation of a confession of faith between the churches: It would be a mistake to attempt to construct a new confession of faith, common to all, which makes an abstraction of the doctrinal tradition of each church. Rather, the surest way to ecumenical reception and consensus regarding the one faith is that characterized by mutual respect for legitimate differences, even at the doctrinal level. But this respect must be grounded on the mutual conviction in faith of the existence of genuine personal and communitarian charisms which inspire the differences, without damaging the unity of faith.

III. Conclusion

In the ancient Catholic Church the process of reception of the resolutions of ecumenical councils had these common characteristics: The testing of the claim of the council to hand on the consensus of the church past and present led to a spiritual assimilation of the conciliar teaching which made a real difference in the daily life of faith of each church and fostered a deepening of the awareness of the unity existing between the receiving churches. In addition, the integration of the conciliar dogmas into the global perception of the faith produced a new synthesis which often affected credal formulations.

The four questions posed by the Faith and Order Commission for official responses of the churches to the Lima text seem to be inspired by, or at least correspond to, this reception process. There are also many analogies between the reception process of the common heritage reflected in the Lima text and that which took place in the dialogue between the participants of an ecumenical council. Finally, mention can be made of the relative imperfections of the Lima text and resolutions of ecumenical councils from the viewpoint of elaboration of doctrine and difficulties arising from a supposed theological direction which may seem to favor one or another church tradition. But there is a crucial difference between the Lima text and the decisions of an ecumenical council, which is particularly relevant to the reception process as understood by Faith and Order: The architects of the Lima text acted as responsible, competent individual representatives for their church traditons, while the participants of an ecumenical council acted as official representatives of the churches with the mission to make a decision about the faith on their behalf. Two observations on this difference may suffice to bring this discussion of reception in history to a close.

First, the ecumenical council was an event of the one communion of churches and recognized as such. When it took a position on an essential issue, it placed a theological act of faith, hope, and love. The meaning of the decision remained, in the consciousness of all who agreed with it, inseparable from the spiritual event lived by all in the council. Hence, the first four ecumenical councils, for example, were confident that their definitions provided a commentary on the Creed and could be incorporated into it. This points to the importance of a general council of all churches as the indispensable vehicle for carrying through the reception process begun by Faith and Order.

Second, it is doubtful that a universal council of all Christian churches, or the majority of them, can be realized before the churches actually begin to practice together the life of faith in the areas of common witness to the gospel in charitable works and preaching of the word of God, as well as in common public worship. Through this ecumenical practice of the faith it may be expected that the churches will experience their profound unity in Christ—and so their separation—as something which deeply affects the life of faith in all churches.

It is the common practice of the faith which both enables the churches to recognize one another as "sister" churches and, at the same time, fosters the sense of incompleteness of the life of faith as long as the separation persists. Certainly the development of theological principles is necessary in the quest for the establishment of visible communion between separated churches, but practice of the faith will finally decide what must be done. Practice illuminates; practice tells the truth. It is practice which evokes the experience of the intimate relationship that exists among the churches of Jesus Christ. This follows from the fact that Christian truth is not a matter of abstract principles for life. It exists in the doing of the faith, grounded on the gospel of love.

Through the common practice of the faith it may be hoped that the churches will come to receive one another as faithful to the apostolic tradition according to their lights. At a distance one church may judge that a particular position of another church has not yet reached its goal, but in the common practice of the faith it may be recognized that what is not said by way of dogmatic formulation is already affirmed at the level of the daily life of faith. This will be judged as more significant than the fact that it has not yet been crystallized under the form of a dogma. In the climate nourished by the common practice of faith, the separated churches may move to that experience of communion which allows them to counsel together as one communion of churches after the model of the ancient Catholic Church's general councils. They may even be prepared to affirm together the same faith while respecting the diversity of traditions, after the model of the Council of Florence.

THE LIMA STATEMENT AND THE ORTHODOX

Thomas Hopko

Orthodox reaction to the Lima statement on *Baptism, Eucharist, and Ministry* (hereafter, BEM) has been overwhelmingly positive. There appear to be at least three reasons for this.

The Orthodox are pleased with BEM, first, because they find the statement, both in spirit and content, to be, simply, a very good one. What is said, Orthodox commentators generally believe, and the way it is said are basically sound and right. The document presents a view of baptism, eucharist, and ministry with which the Orthodox can for the most part heartily agree. It clearly indicates areas where further study and clarification are required, and it points up issues where obvious disagreements and difficulties persist. As a "consensus statement" on the present state of affairs concerning the issues in question, the Lima statement is considered by the Orthodox, as I see it, to be remarkably successful.

A second reason that the Orthodox are happy with BEM in my observation is that the statement comes from a body of theologians who, if not officially representing their respective churches, are still confirmed in their work by their ecclesiastical leadership in an official manner. Since virtually all Christian confessions are represented in the composition of BEM, including many which are not members of the World Council of Churches, such as the Roman Catholics (who are, however, officially members of the W.C.C. Faith and Order Commission), the Lima statement becomes the most inclusive and most official ecumenical Christian statement on its theme ever produced. For this reason alone, Orthodox commentators believe it is to be received and responded to with the greatest respect.

A third reason that the Orthodox are pleased with BEM is that they have always insisted that faith and order, and doctrine and worship, are at the very heart of ecclesiastical life and ecumenical activity. They have held the position

Thomas Hopko (Orthodox) is an Associate Professor of Theology at St. Vladimir's Orthodox Theological Seminary, Crestwood, NY, where he has taught since 1968, and Adjunct Professor of Religion at Columbia University. He has a B.A. and a Ph.D. (1982) from Fordham University, an M.Div. from St. Vladimir's Seminary, and an M.A. from Duquesne University. Ordained a priest in the Orthodox Church in 1963 and an archpriest in 1970, he has served as a pastor in three churches in Ohio and New York, and has taught at Duquesne University. A member of the Faith and Order Commission of the World Council of Churches since 1975, Fr. Hopko's most recent books include *All the Fullness of God* (St. Vladimir's Seminary Press, 1982) and *Women and the Priesthood* (editor) (St. Vladimir's, 1983). His articles have appeared in *St. Vladimir's Theological Quarterly, Commonweal, Diakonia, Worship, Spiritual Life, The Orthodox Church*, and several other journals.

since the beginnings of the modern ecumenical movement—in which they have always enthusiastically participated (though never without frustration, confusion, and serious difficulties, both among themselves and with—and for—others)—that the movement is primarily, if not exclusively, for the purpose of bringing divided Christians into doctrinal and sacramental unity in the one church of Christ. Cooperation, where possible, in mission and evangelism and in social action and charitable works has always been blessed by the Orthodox as of critical importance, but of greatest importance is the essential unity of all Christians in the one, apostolic faith of Jesus Christ, which is expressed and participated in in the sacramental and liturgical life of the one church which he has established. For divided, disordered, disagreeing Christians to be united in one body, with one mind and one mouth, they must be brought to the point where their baptismal, eucharistic, and ministerial beliefs and actions are substantially, though not necessarily formally, the same. The publication of BEM, which is as much a doctrinal as it is a sacramental, ritual, and practical statement, takes up this issue and places it squarely before the churches. This fact alone, especially considering the authorship of the document, makes Orthodox hearts rejoice. They believe that a very special "moment of truth" has arrived, what Geoffrey Wainwright has called a "critical" moment in every sense of the word—a moment of judgment and a moment of decision. How the churches react and respond to the Lima statement will reveal where they really stand and where their interests really lie. "Where your treasure is, there will your heart be also." BEM will demonstrate with little doubt where the churches' treasures and hearts are. For this to be made plain at this moment in history, at least for the Orthodox, is of greatest importance and significance.

Questions for the Churches

Three questions are commonly raised by the Orthodox regarding possible reaction to the Lima statement by the Roman Catholic and particularly the Protestant churches. One has to do with the ability of the various bodies to respond to the statement in an authoritative, unified manner. Many Orthodox are of the opinion that most Protestant churches, and perhaps even the Roman Catholic Church, are no longer capable of acting authoritatively as churches because they have lost the sense of "collegiality" within their membership, what the Slavs call "sobornost" (the ability to act in harmony, freely and voluntarily, with one mind and mouth, on issues of faith and worship), and have no hierarchical structure capable of acting decisively in the name of all the believers of the given community. Such a concern, of course, may be directed at the Orthodox themselves, but most Orthodox church leaders and theologians are confident that the doctrinal and liturgical identity shared by all the Orthodox (referring here, of course, to the Byzantine-Chalcedonian churches), together with their clearly hierarchical structure which calls the respective episcopal synods of the self-governing churches to voice their church's official response, should guarantee a unified position on the part of all, despite their greatly, and gravely, differing cultural, social, and political situations in this world.

Another concern of the Orthodox is that some churches may choose to give an interpretation to the Lima statement which will allow them to subscribe to its words while providing a meaning quite consciously known to be different from what the text intends to say and what other church bodies are believed to defend and practice. In a word, the worry here is that each church will interpret BEM in its own way, while freely acknowledging, if not actually encouraging, others to do the same, claiming that this is in any case all that can be done and the only thing to be done, if the document is going to be received by the churches in a way that will result in the mutual recognition and common sacramental worship which may, one day, lead to ultimate unification. With one voice, the Orthodox have always opposed such an approach to ecumenical activity. They have consistently insisted that, while words, symbols, and rites may legitimately vary among Christian churches, the meaning which they convey and celebrate must be one and the same. Otherwise, there is factually no unity, but a mere facade which is nominal and contrived, and which ultimately is false and deceiving.

The greatest anxiety found among Orthodox commentators of the Lima statement is that some churches will not treat it at all seriously because they consider the issues with which it deals to be secondary and unimportant. A measure of cynicism may even enter at this point, if not open contempt and hostility toward those who hold BEM to be of critical significance. This may result in responses, or the absence of responses, which will gravely obstruct, if not totally destroy, the chance for unity among Christians as understood and desired by the Orthodox. Thus, there are Orthodox who fear not only that some churches will prove themselves unable to respond to BEM as churches, and others which may do so merely in a formal manner, but also that others may treat the whole effort with indifference, cynicism, or outright contempt. As stated above, however, even to know this has its advantage, according to the Orthodox.

Specific Issues of Concern

In addition to the general concerns about the Lima statement raised by the Orthodox, several specific issues arise when its various parts are examined. In the section on baptism, the greatest concern has to do with the distinction and relationship between baptism and chrismation; the relationship of baptism and chrismation to the eucharist; and the place of children, particularly infants, relative to these sacraments. The Orthodox hold that baptism by immersion is a person's

Easter (*Pascha*) and that chrismation, which is a person's Pentecost, must necessarily accompany baptism in every instance as a distinct act. As Christ and the Spirit are not the same, yet never separated, and as the passover of Christ's death and resurrection is distinct from the coming of the Holy Spirit, yet never divided from it, so baptism and chrismation (which is not easily identified with the "confirmation" of any of the Western churches, varying as the understandings and practices are) must also always be united with appropriate theological, liturgical, and spiritual distinctions which allow each act to be what it is in harmony with the other. The Orthodox generally find the baptism statement greatly lacking at this point.

There is also a lack of clarity about the relationship of baptism (and chrismation) to the eucharist. The Orthodox hold that baptized (and chrismated) people, including infants, are led directly and necessarily to the eucharistic table for Holy Communion. They find it incomprehensible that a baptized person would be denied access to the eucharist. And if "confirmations" of various sorts are to parallel Orthodox "chrismation," then the communion of a person before or without "confirmation" would be problematic for the Orthodox, not to say outright unacceptable. Here, as we shall see again, the case of children is of particular importance.

The Orthodox also are displeased about the language of "believers'" and "nonbelievers'" baptism. They do not consider it appropriate to label children as "nonbelievers," especially those who are members of believing families and/or are in the care of and share their lives with believing adults. They hold that children in the latter circumstances must be baptized (and so partake of the eucharist) if they are to develop normally as persons in community, both Christian and "human." There is no valid reason, in Orthodox opinion, for excluding such children from full participation in the gracious life of Christ's church. They see in the behavior of children in such circumstances signs of willing participation in the church's sacramental life in no sense different from or inferior to that of retarded or senile adults—not to speak of the nominal, cynical, indifferent, or plainly unworthy adult members who participate sacramentally in virtually all the churches. The issue of children is neither small nor secondary for the Orthodox. It is of crucial importance not only in respect to the sacraments but also in respect to Christian understandings and practices regarding childhood and children. It is also, as we shall see, of paramount importance for the Orthodox themselves in regard to their own "domestic," as well as "ecumenical," behavior.

The issues that emerge among the Orthodox relative to the eucharist when considering Roman Catholic and Reformed responses to BEM are those having to do primarily with what can be called the modern "Western" language, categories, and problematics in which the section is generally cast. There is still a lack of attention to the essential connection between the eucharist and the very being of the church as it is constituted and structured in time and space. There is still a reduction of the eucharistic mystery to what happens to the bread and the wine, rather than to what happens to the whole of the gathering, not to speak of the whole church, and of creation itself. There is still the use of such problematic and, for the Orthodox, nontraditional expressions as "real presence," and such ambiguous categories as that of "sign." How the eucharist is a sacrifice, if indeed it is, must yet be clarified, together with other critical issues, such as the relationship of the leader of the eucharistic action to the ordained ministry and to the nonordained members of the royal priesthood of all believers. There is also, as we have seen and will see again, the issue of the relationship of the eucharist to baptism (and chrismation), particularly in regard to infants and young children.

For the Orthodox the eucharist is the actualization of the church in the time and space of this age and this world. It is the "locus" of the church's self-expression and self-constitution, the "place" where the church becomes itself, proclaiming, celebrating, and experiencing its gospel, its doctrine, its scriptural interpretation, its vision of reality, its very being and life as God's final, covenanted community with creation—the mystical and sacramental actualization on earth, here and now, of that kingdom of God which will come in power at the end of the world in the *parousia* of Christ. As such, the church is not just the *anamnesis* (remembrance) and anticipation of God's kingdom. Nor is the church merely its effective "sign." Rather, the church is its very *presence*, here and now, which presence is revealed in the eucharistic mystery in which not only the bread and wine, but the very gathering itself, becomes "holy communion," the body of Christ. The Lima statement tends to such a view, according to most of its Orthodox interpreters, and they appreciate it sincerely. But, according to them, its scriptural, apostolic, early Christian, and traditionally Christian affirmations remain obstructed and distorted by the Reformation/Counter-Reformation problematics and categories with which it deals and according to which it is still for the most part formulated.

The section on the ministry, according to most Orthodox examiners, suffers the same weaknesses. Its fundamental approach is sound, and its intentions are good, but its attempt to formulate a clear distinction between the ordained ministry and the ministry of the nonordained, between the ordained priests and the "priesthood of all believers"—both of which are rooted in the unique high priesthood of Christ and are each, in their own ways, expressions of it—remains ambiguous in what it proposes practically for reception by the churches. The longest of the sections, it obviously deals with the most difficult issues not only theologically, but also practically, bureaucratically, and personally. Church organizations and living people are directly involved. Their rights and their privileges, as well as their pay and their power, are directly called into question. The hardest and most divisive issue has to do with the ministerial ordination of women, which raises questions not only about the priesthood and episcopate but

also about the very nature of human beings as created in God's image and likeness. In a word, the issue here is about God, and so about Christianity, the
church, and life itself. The Orthodox generally hold that the answer to the questions about the ordination of women contains the answers to all theological
questions. Until now, the Orthodox have unanimously opposed the ordination
of women to the presbyterate and episcopate, while searching for an appropriate
theological explanation for their position. It does not appear at all likely, with
or without an accepted theological formulation on the subject, that the Orthodox are prepared to recognize their own faith and life in any church which has
ordained women ministers.

Judgment on the Orthodox

While the Orthodox generally believe that the Lima statement will be more
difficult to deal with for the Protestant churches than for themselves or the
Roman Catholics, both in regard to its content and to its call for official and
authoritative response, it is clear that the document confronts the Orthodox
with many serious questions and difficult decisions.

It remains to be seen, first of all, how seriously the statement will be taken
by the Orthodox churches, including their theologians and people, and how far
Orthodox leaders are willing to go in recognizing the sacramental teachings and
practices of other Christian bodies as compatible in essence, if not in form,
with their own. This issue exacerbates a strong debate already raging among the
Orthodox. While all Orthodox churches without exception are members of the
World Council of Churches and participate in ecumenical activity, deep and serious questioning has always existed among the Orthodox about the nature and
significance of this participation and activity. This questioning has become more
intense in recent years because of the radical changes which have occurred in
theological and moral teachings and practices, as well as in sacramental ritual,
discipline, and behavior within most Western churches—including here, in the
first instance, the Roman Catholic Church.

While some Orthodox claim that the Lima statement reflects the fruit of
sound ecumenical theologizing and a return to sense and serious ecumenical activity, after what they see to be the secularizing and relativizing captivity of the
ecumenical Christian world since the 1960's, there are others who claim that
the doctrinal, moral, and spiritual decomposition of the Western churches which
has occurred at this time—whatever the handful of professional theologians who
produced BEM have to say—compels the Orthodox to proceed with extreme
caution in offering any sort of recognition of Christian belief and behavior in
these bodies. The Orthodox have to reach a clear decision in this matter. To
what extent are Western Christians Christian? If there is indeed something of

Christ and *the* church in their churches, which virtually all Orthodox are willing to admit, how is this recognized and affirmed in practice, and what does it mean for the unity of Christians in the one church of Christ, which all Orthodox believe to be the Orthodox Church? This issue is not only an incredibly complicated one, but it is also of critical spiritual significance for the Orthodox. They will answer before God for how they resolve it.[1]

In addition to the general call to decision concerning the non-Orthodox which the Lima statement presents to the Orthodox, the document makes several specific points of judgment on Orthodox beliefs and practices. The Orthodox insist, for example, that it is proper to baptize infants in the care of believing adults (doing so by immersion) and to bring them to Holy Communion at the eucharistic gathering. It is well known, however, that this is done in most churches with little or no preparation. The baptizing priest or bishop often does not even know the names of the people, both parents and sponsors, who bring children for baptism and communion—not to mention their actual religious belief and moral behavior. The same holds true for participation in the eucharist. In some churches the practice of confession of sins and spiritual openness to one's brothers and sisters in the Lord, or at least minimally to one's pastor, has completely disappeared. If these were merely matters of laxity or decadence, there would, for ecumenical purposes, be no great difficulty. The problem, however, is that such behavior is sometimes ideologically defended, even by church leaders, which makes the testimony of the Lima statement, and what it implies for mutual recognition, much more judging upon the Orthodox. For how can the Orthodox demand from others for the sake of recognition what it does not demand from its own members, not only in practice, but even in theory?

The issue about the baptism, chrismation, and participation of infants in Holy Communion presents another even greater difficulty. We have seen how Orthodox commentators on the Lima statement stress the fact that baptism, chrismation, and communion essentially go together, even for infants. The impli-

---

[1]There are people in all Orthodox churches (as well as entire groups not in communion with the Orthodox patriarchates and self-governing churches, such as the so-called "Russian Orthodox Church outside Russia [the "Synod"]," and the "True Greek Orthodox Church"), who hold that there is nothing of Christ outside the Orthodox Church, and certainly no sacraments. These people claim that the non-Orthodox must be treated as pagans, if not as demon-riddled apostates, and must be exorcised and baptized if they wish to enter the Orthodox Church. This is obviously not the official position of any of the Orthodox churches, all of which participate in the W.C.C. and in ecumenical activity generally. Nor is it the position of many Orthodox Christians who seriously question Orthodox membership in the W.C.C. and in the National Council of the Churches of Christ in the U.S.A. as proper and beneficial because of the traditional Orthodox understanding of the nature of church unity, as well as their views concerning Christian, and particularly *ecclesiastical*, involvement in social and political activities—not to speak of the actual policies and actions in these areas presently conducted by W.C.C. and N.C.C.C. leadership, which virtually all Orthodox, for a variety of reasons, find almost totally unacceptable.

cation is that the churches which do not have such a belief and practice cannot be recognized by the Orthodox and that the Orthodox cannot have sacramental fellowship with them. It is a well-known fact, however, that there are whole dioceses within the canonical unity of Orthodox patriarchates where infants are regularly baptized by pouring or sprinkling water and are excluded from participation in the Holy Eucharist until they make their first confession at about the age of eight or nine. This practice which is found among those who have been heavily influenced in Europe by Roman Catholic theology and discipline, most of whom are of Eastern-rite Catholic backgrounds, is often not simply accommodated by pastoral *oikonomia*, but is defended by those who do it as a legitimate practice, indeed even as the proper practice, for Christians.

The issue here is clear. If such is the case (whether it is a pastoral accommodation or a legitimate practice is irrelevant), how can the Orthodox possibly retain full canonical union and sacramental communion with these people, while at the same time criticizing and refusing to recognize the same practices in others outside its canonical boundaries? The Orthodox are obliged to answer this question for themselves, first of all, as well as for others.

There are many other questions which the Orthodox have to answer in responding to the Lima statement. How, for example, can the Orthodox insist that baptism, with chrismation and communion, is a communal event involving the whole church when it is almost always performed semiprivately in a perfunctory manner with but a small group of people attending, very often in the case of a newborn infant (because of gross misunderstandings of church discipline and tradition) in the absence of the child's own mother? How can the Orthodox insist on the centrality of the eucharist in church life when in so many places the laity (and nonofficiating clergy) do not participate regularly in the sacraments, receiving communion but a few times a year, and that with questionable practices of preparation? How can the Orthodox claim that the bishops are the sacramental images of Christ in the church, preserving the unity, identity, and solidarity of the church's faith and life in each place, when in virtually every place in so-called "non-Orthodox countries" there are several bishops who govern not territories of believers, but ethnic enclaves? How can the Orthodox claim collegiality and *sobornost* in church life when so many bishops in so many churches are cut off from their people, who participate only nominally, if at all, in their elections and appointments, and virtually never have the opportunity for common conversation and direct dialogue? How can the Orthodox affirm a multiplicity of ministries in the church when the ministry of lay people, particularly women, is generally so limited and unsupported by hierarchical and bureaucratic structures, and even by the populace at large? And if the Orthodox oppose the ordination of women to the presbyterate and episcopate, are they prepared to give a good defense of this position which will be convincing to those who are willing to listen? These and many other questions confront the Orthodox who expose themselves to the Lima statement and allow themselves to be questioned by it.

These questions generally embrace three areas: (1) Are the Orthodox able to show in fact, through their actual practices, what their formal doctrines and discipline, their official "faith and order," require? And, if not, what does this mean for the recognition of others who also deviate from Orthodox ways? (2) Are the Orthodox willing to tolerate in others, for the sake of Christian unity, the same sorts of deficiencies and deviations which they are obviously willing to tolerate in many of their own members? And, if not, why not? (3) Are the Orthodox capable of providing clear and convincing explanations of their positions and practice for the people of goodwill outside their churches who are confused and disturbed by Orthodox belief and behavior? These appear to be the kinds of questions which the Lima statement is asking of the Orthodox churches. It now remains to be seen how, if at all, they will be answered.

CHICAGO THEOLOGIANS ON BEM

Robert W. Bertram

Since the N.C.C.'s BEM conference in Chicago in October, 1983, was co-hosted by an ecumenical cooperative of Chicago-area theological schools, it was natural that these schools would contribute to the conference a public review of BEM's theology. This they did in two successive panel discussions, each involving three Chicago faculty members: Lauree Hersch Meyer of Bethany Theological Seminary on "Baptism," O. C. Edwards of Seabury-Western Theological Seminary on "Eucharist," Lewis Mudge of McCormick Theological Seminary on "Ministry"; and Bernard McGinn of the University of Chicago's Divinity School on "Baptism," Carolyn Osiek of Catholic Theological Union on "Ministry," Robert Bertram of Lutheran School of Theology at Chicago on "Eucharist."

Although the panelists were to address the substantive issues of baptism, eucharist, and ministry, not the conference theme of "reception" as such, what they said about BEM's theological substance had implications for its reception process as well. Two implications in particular deserve notice. The two I have in mind are not the obvious twosome, which every panelist also reflected: yes, BEM is already basically receivable; no, it is not to be received uncritically or even without further revision. That much yes-and-no was reflected even by the two panelists from the Faith and Order Commission, Mudge and Bertram, who at Lima had already gone on record in BEM's favor, so now leaned over backward to add a "critical response" as Moderator Carl Braaten requested.

But, beyond such general endorsement cum "critical evaluation," which BEM's own preface invites, all six panelists surfaced two other, more nuanced, more telling features of BEM's theology, which in turn might foreshadow how the document will be received in the churches: first, BEM's theological ambivalences—or, better, its inconclusiveness—and, second, its intimations of something better still to come.

Robert W. Bertram (Lutheran) is Seminex Professor of Historical and Systematic Theology at the Lutheran School of Theology at Chicago. He attended Concordia Seminary, St. Louis, and the University of Chicago (M.A. and Ph.D.). He had a Fulbright to the University of Munich on three occasions, at both the Catholic and Protestant theological faculties, and has lectured at the University of Bergen, Norway. A leader in the formation of "Seminex," Dr. Bertram is a member of the W.C.C. Faith and Order Commission and of the Lutheran-Roman Catholic Consultation in the U.S.A. He is a contributor to C. Braaten (ed.), *The New Church Debate* (Fortress, 1983), and E. Lorenz (ed.), *Politik als Glaubenssache* (Lutheran World Federation, 1983).

Inconclusive

First, in noting BEM's inconclusiveness, I would not minimize that the document did evince definite conclusions from our panelists. The conclusions they drew, however, all of them apparently warranted by BEM itself, occasionally were not just different. They were at times markedly contrary, leaving the audience in a quandary and the discussion as a whole undecided. That sort of irresolution may be a shadow of things to come. All the more so, if, as this conference recommended, a document such as BEM which has been ecumenically produced ought also, as in these Chicago panels, to be ecumenically discussed and received. The fallout from any reception process as multivocal as that may be a whole new range of interesting theological impasses.

For instance, contrast the two presentations by Hersch Meyer and Edwards, she from Church of the Brethren, he an Episcopalian. Both affirmed BEM for reasons of their own, but for reasons not evidently compatible with each other. Hersch Meyer explained that, for Brethren, "baptism was never understood as a means of saving one's soul." Rather it functions as a rite of passage into the religious group, thus fulfilling an important sociological need of both the person and the community. It is only of secondary importance that the "socio-ecclesial formation terrain" of the Brethren had traditionally limited this rite to adults. Recently there has been a growing recognition that adolescents, too, need a rite of passage. At that, "a meaningful adolescent rite need not be confirmation or baptism any more than a meaningful infant rite needs to be baptism or infant dedication." What matters is "enrolling each new generation meaningfully in the corporate identity."

Such a "free church" view of baptism would seem to justify the misgivings voiced by Edwards. Not that he had serious doubts about BEM. On the contrary, he could comfortably acknowledge that "the Lima statement does presuppose a sacramental orientation that is reflexive to Anglicanism, and the thought world of the statement feels like our native land." No, he explained,

> My questions about this as an adequate basis for reunion lie outside the document. My question is whether many of the member churches of the World Council who have not been so sacramental in their orientation throughout history as Anglicans have are really this converted to a sacramental point of view.

As Edwards went on, his real question lay deeper: "The sacramentalism of the Lima statement implies a Christology on a par with the classic christological statements of the early church." Must not those creeds, therefore, be "an essential part of any discussion of reunion?" What he wondered, not optimistically, was whether "all the member churches are willing to ascribe such an ultimacy to Christ."

Hersch Meyer, whose Brethren obviously have "not been so sacramental in their orientation throughout history as Anglicans have," and maybe not so

inclined "to ascribe such ultimacy to Christ," nevertheless argued from an explicitly christological orientation of her own. The Christian community into which
baptism provides a rite of passage is, after all, "the body of Christ," and membership in it means "participation in Christ's very life." "What social scientists
would call a sociological" event is what "Brethren would understand as an incarnational" one. Indeed, Hersch Meyer's single most theological reason for approving BEM is its "christological mode" of "Christian conversation," but by that
she meant, "Christians today are learning to see in others who practice radically
different forms of baptism . . . members of Christ's living body, incarnated in
a social matrix sometimes painfully and astonishingly different from our own."

   If that is what strikes Hersch Meyer as christologically significant about
BEM, namely, its "openness to expression of God's Spirit visibly different from
our own," then she was being consistent in challenging the way the BEM question is frequently posed: "the question to what degree the document adequately
represents the apostolic faith." "That very wording," she objected, "suggests to
Brethren . . . a view of 'correspondence' more than 'relational' truth." And
Edwards' plea, by contrast, for "a Christology on a par with the classic christological statements of the early church" must then sound like the very thing
Hersch Meyer criticized as a "search for a particular deposit . . . to rightly
represent the faith."

   Still, BEM evidently seems inclusive enough to embrace Brethren as well.
Both their "faith and practice," says Hersch Meyer, "is found within those de-
scriptions the BEM document affirms." Edwards, however, questions whether
churches such as Hersch Meyer's truly can find themselves there. She, in turn,
questions whether his sort of criterion is worthy of BEM, also christologically.
"It's the old question of the Council of Florence," Mudge observed. "How do
you know that when you use different words you are speaking with the same
intention?" (Or even, we might ask, when you use the *same* words?) Edwards:
"And the Catch-22 of all this is that in order to deal with the questions we are
faced with we must first reach some sort of methodological agreement so that
we will know that we are talking about the same thing." The discussion then
digressed farther and farther from the theological issues at hand (baptism, eucharist, and ministry) toward some elusive "hermeneutical" solution—toward a solution, in other words, outside BEM itself, though necessitated by BEM's own
theological indeterminateness.

   BEM's inconclusiveness did not need interdenominational give-and-take to
reveal it, though that helped. It surfaced right within panelists' solo presentations, for instance, in McGinn's and Osiek's, both of them Roman Catholic lay
theologians. McGinn was "puzzled . . . about the nature and content of [BEM's]
new ethical orientation granted in baptism." Why "puzzled"? "Because the text
says so little about what used to be called original sin," upon which any such
conclusions about baptismal renewal would presumably need to be premised.
Other points of puzzlement for McGinn were the relation of baptism to faith,
as well as baptism's sacramental causality: "If there are still differences of theo-

logical interpretation under the fairly calm surface of the document that imply real differences of belief, I do not think that the document itself tells us how to deal with them.

Or Osiek, on BEM's treatment of ministry: "The traditional tension remains between the theology of charism and the act of ordination; the tension is *not* resolved by simply assuming as 1 Tim. 4:14 seems to that ordained ministry *is* a charism." As for the apostolicity of ordained ministries, she observed, "There is no more obvious sign of compromise in the document than the conclusion of #10: 'There is therefore a difference between the apostles and the ordained ministers whose ministries are founded on theirs.' That there is a difference no one would dispute. Apparently every attempt to articulate what *kind* of difference was unsuccessful."

Mudge, similarly, called attention to BEM's unresolved tensions, including one which the document itself acknowledges: ". . . the degree of the presbyter's participation in the episcopal ministry is still for many an unresolved question of far-reaching ecumenical importance"—far-reaching enough, I might insert, to exercise Lutherans. Recalling Lima, Mudge was inclined to trace some of BEM's lingering tensions back to its prepublication "drafting process." He remembered how free-church and Reformed theologians "felt we were always tugging at cassocks to get heard. . . . I do wonder sometimes whether our Orthodox friends, particularly those who are resident in Eastern Europe and the Soviet Union and Greece, have any real understanding of what Protestantism is . . . and what we mean in the West by the critical method."

The critical method came up also in Bertram's challenge to BEM, specifically with respect to its chapter on "the institution of the eucharist." Here again was a case where the document is "halting between two opinions," needlessly so. For one example (and there were several), BEM at first gives the appearance of affirming the apostolic tradition that the sacrament was instituted by the historical Jesus. Then, "needlessly cautious," BEM retreats from that doctrinally crucial claim, apparently fearing that a dominical institution may no longer be tenable, which to say the least is a premature conclusion. As a result, rather than grapple with "historical-critical evidence," which in this case might just have supported the apostolic tradition, BEM "shifts the dominical origins of the eucharist instead to Jesus' general practice throughout his ministry of table fellowship." But, at what a price, "thus obscuring how precisely in his *new* supper Jesus does *not* eat and drink with his disciples, and obscuring *why* he does not."

Anticipatory

If BEM gives off mixed signals, especially when these are tricked out in mixed theological company, it seems to do so in a way that does not at all stultify further effort. On the contrary, if our panelists' reactions were typical, BEM awakens expectations which point beyond the document in its present form, perhaps beyond anything that is so far conceivable. In that sense BEM is proleptic, self-eclipsing, anticipatory of better things to come, as the following excerpts from the panelists' presentations illustrate:

McGinn: The Lima statement obviously is looking for something more than mutual toleration. It does say that it intends to be an expression of the common faith of the church, and it asks for the explicit mutual recognition of each other's baptism on the part of the churches. But each of these express intentions contains hidden ambiguities that make the process of reception (or nonreception) at least as important as the document.

The Lima document appears to have done as much as it could have within a particular set of circumstances, but perhaps its real hope is that the discussion and debate over its meaning and reception will create a new set of circumstances, a new reality which will eventually make things that now seem difficult, if not impossible, to resolve far less problematic. I do not want to say that the conversation we are engaged in is the reality we seek, but it is perhaps the best way open to us to move forward so that we may be able to catch some glimpse of what that reality actually may be.

Osiek: On the subject of the relationship of the ordained ministry to the apostles and of the ordained priesthood to the priesthood of all believers, we still have some distance to go, both ecumenically and in the theologizing of the more highly structured churches. The greatest challenge for Roman Catholics, I believe, will be to take this document seriously, not just as an ecumenical statement to tell us what others are thinking, but also as a document in which we see ourselves reflected and to which we look to guide our reflections: a statement to be not only informative but *formative* as well.

A monumental step has been taken with the Lima document. Let us welcome it with appropriate joy as a child born into the world who has thereby begun the long process toward maturity. There is a commonly expressed opinion that the documents of Vatican II represented the state of the question at the time they were written but began to be obsolete as soon as the Council ended. Perhaps that would not be a bad way to view the Lima document as well, so that we can receive it not as an achievement but rather as a call into the future.

Hersch Meyer: I think I would want to speak not so much trying to represent the document . . . as trying to find my way as a member of a free-church tradition *into* the document, meaningfully. That is precisely the reason why I . . . was pressed to use incarnational and christological language. I found no other way to make coherent both my participation and also the limits where I felt participation simply could not occur.

I would go past that, though. We have in our traditions, I think, an orthodoxy which trusts formulations. Some of us are organized more around orthopraxis than around orthodoxy. We trust that as well. In ecumenical dialogue neither of these, when we actually are able to change, is the center of our life. Neither is orthodoxy nor orthopraxis a change of any transformation in our communion. Rather, that happens in the moment when we experience ourselves as *made* one . . . by the Spirit in ways that allow us to question very specific previous forms. To think only in terms of what we *say* and how we shall *there* achieve unity or what we *do* and how we shall *there* achieve unity is not enough. Christological analysis is not enough. Really a trinitarian mode of reflecting on our life in communion together strikes me as utterly basic.

Edwards: I do not think that any Anglican could for a moment believe that the seamless robe of Christ has been restored with the Quakers not in it. The Friends' spirituality is one that has borne an effective witness to us, and in some ways we probably feel more commonality with you [Friends] than with many of the people to whom we are closer in matters of polity. So I could never rest content until our conversations had proceeded much farther along the road.

But, finally, it may be that this ability to reach across differences of tradition can only be done in stages. So, conceivably, only those who are able to live with the kind of point of view of the Lima statement so far could participate in this first stage of discovering what we have in common. But, when we are able to clarify *that* with one another, maybe then a *new* stage of conversation could reach out to those who are in your [Friends'] tradition and others, to find out what *all* of us have in common—with the certainty that the things that unite us are far more important than the things that separate us.

Mudge: I believe that what BEM says about the historic threefold ministry will be very helpful in the negotiations between your [Edwards' Episcopal] church and mine. Presbyterians are beginning to realize that they have at the level of the local congregation what might be called a miniaturization of the historic threefold ministry, in which a bishop or pastor is surrounded by presbyters, whom we call elders, and assisted by deacons. That is, I believe, essentially the Ignatian form of the episcopacy, in which the bishop was the pastor of a congregation. It is a fact that in the nineteenth century, when you look at Presbyterian presbytery rolls, when the attendance was taken, it said, "The following *bishops* were present." The reference was to pastors of congregations. That is an historical memory of our intention in constituting a diocese in each local congregation. If we can see that the differences between our two churches have to do with scale—larger diocese, smaller diocese—rather than with principle, and if we can see that the essentials of the historic threefold ministry can be expressed in varying constitutional or canonical forms, then we have the basis for understanding each other.

Bertram: While it is essential in Holy Communion to stress its intercessory and its thanksgiving (that is, its "eucharistic") action, in short its action as one great prayer to the Father made possible by the joining of our lowly prayers with the efficacious intercessions of our great High Priest, is it not likewise a mark of catholicity, indeed the very height of gratitude, when we, the guests at the Lord's Supper, finally accede to what he has so generously invited us to do in the first place, namely, *sup*? Is not that in fact the essence of the *anamnesis* —that, as he bids us, we *eat and drink*, believing, and, thus, in the most earthy and gustatory way (as befits earthlings) we share in his selfsame cruciform and Eastered flesh? And is it not true that we do that supping explicitly "for the forgiveness of sin" and "for proclaiming the Lord's death till he comes," two powerfully anamnetic themes from the Great Tradition about which BEM says virtually nothing? But it certainly could, and it could do so consistently with its own great starting point, in the eucharist as *anamnesis*.

This weakness which appears in BEM appears only because at that very point the document is being particularly strong and bold, raising the churches' highest expectations, but, then, alas, it slacks off and shrinks from its full apostolic promise. So our "critical evaluation" is really only a part of *receiving* BEM, a way of cheering it on and saying, "Yes, yes, go on; don't stop now."

RECEPTION OF "BAPTISM, EUCHARIST, AND MINISTRY" AND THE APOSTOLIC FAITH STUDY

Geoffrey Wainwright

The primary constitutional aim of the World Council of Churches is to facilitate the search by the churches for "visible unity in one faith and in one eucharistic fellowship." All this is to be done because of Christ's express will and for the sake of proclaiming the gospel to the world, these obediential and evangelistic motives being subsumed in the doxological category of doing all for God's glory (cf. Jn. 17). One faith, one eucharistic fellowship: those are the expression, the modalities, the conditions of the visible unity to which the churches are called. The Faith and Order Commission and the Faith and Order Secretariat of the World Council of Churches have a special role in keeping this task before the W.C.C. and the churches. And it is clear that the two themes that I am to combine—"Baptism, Eucharist, and Ministry" and "The Apostolic Faith Study" —are central to the concern for one faith and one eucharistic fellowship. My task is to show some relations between those two Faith and Order projects. I will begin with the historic origin of the Apostolic Faith study.

I. The Emergence of the Apostolic Faith Study

Already in *Baptism, Eucharist, and Ministry* (hereafter, BEM), we have the full flower of the 1982 Lima text, and we hope that it will very soon bear fruit. With the Apostolic Faith study only very tiny spots are beginning to appear on the branch. Not much will be said here in description of BEM, since the text is readily accessible. The Preface to the document provides at least an outline of the fifty-five years of work in Faith and Order that went into its production.[1]

---

[1]More of the background can be found in my book, *The Ecumenical Moment: Crisis and Opportunity for the Church* (Grand Rapids: Eerdmans, 1983).

Geoffrey Wainwright (British Methodist) is Professor of Systematic Theology at the Divinity School of Duke University, Durham, NC, and in the Graduate Program in Religion at Duke. He has taught previously at Union Theological Seminary, New York (1979-83), The Queen's College, Birmingham, England (1973-79), and the Protestant Faculty of Theology in Yaoundé, Cameroon (1967-73). He holds an M.A. and B.D. from the University of Cambridge and a Dr. Theol. (1969) from the University of Geneva. A member of the World Council of Churches' Faith and Order Commission, he chaired the working group on the final text of BEM at Lima. An ordained minister, Dr. Wainwright has also served on the Methodist-Roman Catholic bilateral dialogues and is the President of the Societas Liturgica for 1983-85. His most recent books are *Doxology* (Oxford University Press, 1980), *Eucharist and Eschatology* (Oxford, new ed., 1981), and *The Ecumenical Moment* (Eerdman's, 1983).

72   Geoffrey Wainwright

The churches have been engaged all along in the process of working on BEM,
but they have done it by and large through representative theologians whom
they have trusted to express the positions from which the various confessional
traditions are coming to the question. That operation was broadened when the
churches were asked to comment on the Accra draft of 1974, *One Baptism, One
Eucharist, and a Mutually Recognized Ministry*. But, after Lima, we are now at
a stage in which the churches, through their active leadership and through their
congregational life, are being called upon to take a more explicit and obvious
part in the BEM project. It may seem odd, if in these circumstances we start
immediately with what appears to be something new, the Apostolic Faith study.
It would be a natural reaction if people said, "We've only just started to come
to grips with BEM, and now you're wanting to thrust something new on us." It
is important, therefore, to understand the proper relationship between these two
projects.

    The Apostolic Faith study is nothing strictly new. It, too, found expression
in an incipient way at Lausanne, the very first world conference on Faith and
Order, in 1927. The report from Section IV, received without dissent by the
whole meeting, includes these words:

> Notwithstanding the differences in doctrine among us, we are united
> in a common Christian Faith which is proclaimed in the Holy Scrip-
> tures and is witnessed to and safeguarded in the Ecumenical Creed,
> commonly called the Nicene, and in the Apostles' Creed, which
> Faith is continuously confirmed in the spiritual experience of the
> Church of Christ.

If we could take that as being already true and not just the statement of an ideal,
there would be no need for an Apostolic Faith study; everything would already
be achieved. But, the point is this is somewhat ideal language, as the reference
to doctrinal differences betrays, not to mention the implicit contrast with the
visible *dis*continuities of Christian history. The Lausanne sentence is really *looking forward* to a time when we shall be able to confess with one mind and voice
the common scriptural faith to which the classical symbols of the church bear
testimony. So, then, the Apostolic Faith has been an underlying concern of
Faith and Order in its fifty-six years of existence, and it should be seen as setting
the larger context for the BEM project. It is not something new or something
separate. Rather, BEM should be viewed as part of the larger project which is
now being seen in its fullest, most comprehensive character as the question of
the Apostolic Faith.

    Let me relate in a somewhat anecdotal way the recent stages of the Apos-
tolic Faith study. It can be said to begin in its contemporary form at the Nairobi Assembly of the W.C.C. in 1975. The Nairobi Assembly called on the
churches "to undertake a common effort to receive, reappropriate, and confess
together" (those three verbs are all important), "as contemporary occasion requires, the Christian truth and faith delivered through the apostles and handed

down through the centuries." These are the terms of our study. We are concerned with the Apostolic Faith, and we are concerned with the expression of that faith today as contemporary occasion requires. All this task was put by Nairobi under the heading of the "commonly acknowledged authority of God's word."

In June of 1978, a meeting took place in Venice under the auspices of the Joint Working Group between the World Council of Churches and the Roman Catholic Church. A handful of us from each side—from the Faith and Order Commission of the W.C.C. and from the Vatican Secretariat for Christian Unity —produced what became Faith and Order Paper No. 100, *Towards a Confession of the Common Faith.* The procedural importance of this is that the Roman Catholic Church, already represented by theologians who are full members in the Faith and Order Commission of the W.C.C., has played an especially active part from the beginning of concentrated study on the Apostolic Faith. Perhaps the most important substantial point of the Venice document was its recognition of the contribution made, after the normative apostolic period, by the "building period" (*période édificatrice*) of the Fathers, the creeds, the birth of the great liturgies, and the great Councils.

After Venice we moved to Bangalore for the full meeting of the Faith and Order Commission in August, 1978. The results from Venice had to be integrated into the work of the section entitled "Towards Communion in One Faith." I was not a member of that section at Bangalore, being busy rather on BEM, but by all accounts the Apostolic Faith section was a bit of a roughhouse. Naturally enough, perhaps, in that Indian location, there was tension between those from the historic Western churches who might readily think in "Greek conceptualities" and in terms of ancient creeds and those members of the Commission from third-world countries who were concerned lest we avoid the "real issues" of life in the world today. There was a considerable clash as to how one goes about confessing the Apostolic Faith today. Should one begin with the given classical creeds, or should one begin from contemporary questions and situations? To some extent that clash remains, in a more polite form, in the study up to this day. It has come to be realized that the two sets of data must somehow become mutually illuminating, but difference in starting point continues to affect approaches to the task. One substantial contribution taken up by that section at Bangalore was the suggestion of using Eph. 1:3-14 as a scriptural base or reference point.

A meeting of the Standing Commission on Faith and Order took place at Annecy, France, in January, 1981, and it formulated the exact title of the new project: "Towards the Common Expression of the Apostolic Faith Today." In a sense, the whole project will consist in the elaboration of the nuances of that phrase.

We had a busy year in 1981, for in the summer there was a meeting at Chambésy, the Orthodox center outside Geneva, to give firmer shape to this project. It is important to take note of where projects were formulated and developed, because the context of the meeting often affects what comes out of it. And we must, I suppose, trust the providential hand of God in the choice of these places. In the Orthodox context of Chambésy it was firmly decided to put the Niceno-Constantinopolitan Creed at the heart of the Apostolic Faith study. Times can be significant, too, as 1981 was the 1600th anniversary of the Ecumenical Council of Constantinople (381), a circumstance which very precisely called attention to the Niceno-Constantinopolitan Creed.

Meanwhile, a group of us had been meeting in New York and at Princeton to see how the text of BEM, now nearing completion, might be related to its wider context—that of the Apostolic Faith study. Ten or twelve theologians from the area set themselves the modest task of working through BEM in such a way as to detect what elements in it might already be taken as contributing, beyond their own immediate reference, to the Apostolic Faith study in a broader way. We made up a scheme which went through the traditional "topoi" of dogmatic theology: God, humanity, the world, Christ, the Holy Spirit, the church, the last things; then we scanned BEM from that angle, looking for what was explicitly stated or strongly implied or lacking if BEM were to be read as containing the elements of a statement of the Christian faith on the major dogmatic themes.

Then, at Odessa, U.S.S.R., in October, 1981, another consultation of about twenty theologians examined specifically the Niceno-Constantinopolitan Creed and its third article, with concentration on the Holy Spirit. That was again in an Orthodox context, and we were surrounded by the worshiping community of the monastery, the parish, and the seminary, who at their services sang the Nicene Creed to folk tunes—without the *filioque*, of course. We saw what a living part that confession of faith plays in the life of some very simple people in a country where confessing the faith is a costly business. But it was perhaps just this overwhelming Orthodox context and atmosphere that provoked some reactions on the part of Western scholars, and especially Scripture scholars. They asked: How is the Nicene Creed related to Scripture? Are we not making too big a jump in assuming that the Nicene Creed is somehow a kind of summary expression of scriptural truth? We then realized very clearly, if we had not done so before, that a major theme of the Apostolic Faith study would have to be the relationship between the Scriptures and the Nicene Creed.

It was very interesting, however, that at that same meeting we already saw a development among the Orthodox participants. Some Orthodox would be content to say: "The Nicene Creed settles everything. All we need to do is to go on repeating that creed and confessing the faith in those words." That, too, of course, is a problem for the study, because most people do not hold that all we need to do is to continue using those formulas. Most of us would agree that we do need to do that, but also that we need to find new expressions and to face new issues. The interesting development was signalled by the Metropolitan of Kiev, Filaret, in a theological address which recognized that the classical expressions of the Christian faith, though still believed to be true, are conditioned by their time and culture. That was a significant step for a senior Orthodox bishop to make—and especially on his own ground. So we began to have some awareness of the possibility of at least exploring the temporal and cultural conditionings of the confession of faith, both in the past and in our own time and place.

In Lima, in January, 1982, at the next full meeting of the Faith and Order Commission, there was a bit of a storm again over the Apostolic Faith study, and again happily I was out of it, still working on BEM. One of the issues that arose quite forcefully in the working group on the Apostolic Faith, so I am given to understand, was the issue raised from what might loosely be called the "free church" side. In this context, "free churches" are those churches and traditions which historically have a great suspicion of creeds—often because they associate the word "creed" with an oppressive political authority which imposes a creed upon people as a test and expression of unity. Interestingly enough, another development followed: those people who were often shiest with regard to creeds when they are called creeds, nevertheless stand substantially with the Nicene Creed over against those who formally have no difficulty with creeds but kill their content by a thousand qualifications. So another issue came up, which will be with us throughout the study, posed by those liberal Western Protestants for whom the stumbling block is "God from God, light from light, very God from very God." If there is some suspicion with regard to the study in those circles, the underlying motive is the difficulty with the *homoousion*. The battle on that front is with those who are uneasy with trinitarianism.

In any case, Lima reformulated the Nairobi mandate and the three important verbs come back in different ways: to *receive*, to *reappropriate*, and to *confess* together the apostolic faith becomes, in the Lima reformulation:

1. Towards the common *recognition* of the Apostolic Faith as expressed in the ecumenical symbol of that faith, the Nicene Creed.
2. Towards the common *explication* of this Apostolic Faith in the contemporary situation of the churches.
3. Towards a common *confession* of the Apostolic Faith today.[2]

In early October, 1983, after the great interruption of working groups caused by the Vancouver Assembly, we were at last able to meet and begin work, in Rome, on the "Apostolic Faith in the Scriptures and in the Early Church." In a general way, the Rome meeting recognized that the Apostolic Faith study demands a fourfold working method, with all the aspects being mutually involving:

There is, first, the *exegetical* task of determining by means of the scriptural witness the Christian faith concerning God, Christ, the

---

[2]The project, and some papers from preliminary meetings, can be found in Michael Kinnamon, ed., *Towards Visible Unity: Commission on Faith and Order, Lima, 1982*, vol. 2, Faith and Order Paper 113 (Geneva: World Council of Churches, 1982). Note particularly pp. 28-46.

Spirit, the Church, the present life of believers, and the world to come. Second, there are the *historical* tasks of tracing how and why that faith came to find expression in the Nicene-Constantinopolitan Creed, and of determining the relations between that Creed and other formulations of the faith. Third, there is the *hermeneutical* task of reading Scriptures and Creed in our present situations in such ways that the one faith may illuminate our contemporary world. Fourth, there is the ecumenically *constructive* task of finding means and forms by which the faith may today be confessed in praise before God and in witness before our fellow human beings.[3]

My presentation so far has served to locate where we are in the Apostolic Faith project. I now want in briefest outline to show some of the links between BEM and its wider context. There will be three parts to what follows: first, the permanent content of the Apostolic Faith; second, its authoritative proclamation; and third, its contemporary confession.

II. The Relations between BEM and "The Apostolic Faith"

A. The Permanent Content of the Apostolic Faith

1. *The faith confessed in baptism, eucharist, and ministry.* BEM raises the question of what faith it is which is confessed when baptism, eucharist, and ministry are celebrated and practiced. What faith is it into which a person is baptized? What faith is it which is proclaimed in the mode of thanksgiving at the eucharist? What faith is it that ministers are ordained or commissioned to proclaim and on whose basis they exercise their ministry? BEM raises, then, the question of the *content* of the faith. Here it is interesting that the content of the faith is often formulated, on each of those occasions of baptism, eucharist, and ordination, in terms of the *creed*. The Apostles' Creed is quite simply the baptismal profession of faith of the Western church; the Nicene Creed, after a complicated history about which not even scholars are entirely clear, appears before Constantinople to have been a local baptismal creed which was modified by the Council but then gradually became again the baptismal creed of much wider areas in the church, notably in the East, and for a brief period in the West also.[4] So, both the Apostles' and the Nicene Creeds are baptismal confessions of faith. That is one very clear link between BEM and the Apostolic Faith study.

Then, again, at the eucharist, after a slow start, it came to be the case that the Nicene Creed was regularly professed at the celebrations in both East and West, more frequently in some places, less frequently in others. In 1014, Pope Benedict VIII was asked why they did not sing the Creed in the mass at Rome;

---

[3]The Rome report, and a handbook of earlier useful material, are scheduled for publication as Faith and Order Papers.

[4]See J. N. D. Kelly, *Early Christian Creeds*, 3rd ed. (London: Longmans, 1972).

the reply came: "We have not been troubled by heretics and do not need to reassure one another and others of our orthodoxy." It gradually came to be the case that the Nicene Creed took on a kind of doxological role, to be a sung profession of faith at the eucharist. The great eucharistic prayer, which proclaims in thanksgiving the being and acts of God, is another form, somewhat parallel to the creeds, of the confession of the Apostolic Faith.[5]

Again, in ministry, in most churches ordinations include in some shape or form a profession of faith by those who are being ordained. In many cases—and, surprisingly perhaps, even in some Baptist churches—the minister will choose to proclaim his or her faith by using the words of the Nicene Creed. If that is the case even in churches which have historically been suspicious of creeds, it is quite normal that elsewhere some creedal expression, and often the Nicene Creed, should be taken as the faith into which a person is ordained and which a person is ordained to profess.

So, then, BEM and the Apostolic Faith study are related in that way: there is the question of the *content* of the faith in baptism, eucharist, and ministry; and, often in sheer liturgical practice, the creeds or creedlike professions are used.

2. *BEM and the whole range of the Apostolic Faith.* The question hinted at in the New York and Princeton meetings was that of the relation between the BEM document and the whole Apostolic Faith. Here we are on difficult terrain. Some would say that baptism and eucharist and ministry are certainly three important points of Christian doctrine, but they are separable from among (say) twenty-four important points of doctrine. It could then be argued that it is fine to be reaching agreement on these three issues, but we must then go on to all the other twenty-one areas or points of Christian doctrine. That would be one kind of attitude, the "quantitative." Others might say that baptism, eucharist, and ministry are all of it. Once one agrees on that, one has at least implicitly, and perhaps even explicitly, agreed on all that needs to be agreed on in order to have Christian unity. That is the temptation on the more Catholic side of things, especially on the "catholic" wings of Protestant churches, where we have to fight for the importance of these things within our own denominations. That then provokes a reaction, which I met in Rome when I called on my former professor at the Waldensian faculty of theology, Vittorio Subilia, who is a Reformed of the Reformed, and who in this matter simply expresses what is being said by many Latin-language Reformed theologians regarding BEM. They call into question the whole *impostazione*, the whole orientation of this approach, which begins, as they see it, with the sacraments and allows the sacraments then to govern everything which is said about the Christian faith.[6]

---

[5]See, historically, M. Lods, "Préface eucharistique et confession de foi," *Revue d'Histoire et de Philosophie Religieuses* 59 (1979): 121-142.

[6]See, for instance, P. Ricca, "Il 'BEM' e il futuro dell'ecumenismo," *Protestantesimo* 38

There are tensions here, quite evidently, as to how BEM relates to the comprehensive context of the Apostolic Faith. My own inclination would tend to see baptism, eucharist, and ministry—and the agreements in process of being achieved in connection with them—as foci for the wider, more comprehensive theme. BEM does not try to say everything, but it does touch on many topics and gathers together issues having to do with Trinity, with the person and work of Christ, with the nature of the church, with the reign to come, and so on. Therefore, provided one takes them, modestly but really, as foci for the wider questions dealing with the Apostolic Faith, the sacraments and the ministry do represent one entry to the complex of questions, and a positive relation can be established between work on BEM and work on the Apostolic Faith study.

B. The Authoritative Proclamation of the Apostolic Faith

From the Vancouver Assembly, the report on "Steps towards Unity" contains these words:

> The ways in which the churches respond to BEM and the ways in which they engage in a longer process of reception provide an ecumenical context within which the churches can learn to understand and encounter each other's ways of making decisions about church teaching. The significance of this opportunity needs to be emphasized, for common agreement about ways of teaching and decision-making is one of the fundamental marks of church unity.

It is a question of authority: the authoritative decision as to what the Apostolic Faith is, and the authoritative proclamation of that faith. Those issues are necessarily raised by BEM—and very precisely by the question of official response and continuing reception.[7]

1. *The reception of BEM—a case study for the churches.* The response and reception process with regard to BEM offers a kind of case study, a prime example of how the churches, in their divided state, teach authoritatively. Each church, if it will respond to BEM officially, has first of all to decide how it will respond. BEM in its Preface asks that churches respond at "the highest appropriate level of authority." The W.C.C. and the Faith and Order Commission cannot presume to tell the churches what their highest appropriate level of authority is. By the way in which they respond, the churches will indicate to others and to themselves what they consider to be the highest appropriate level of authority, and along the way they will also illustrate what factors go into the shaping of decisions to be taken at the highest appropriate level of authority: what the levels of consultation will be, who the advisors will be, when and where

---

(1983): 155-169.

[7]One of the earlier studies referred to is "How Does the Church Teach Authoritatively Today?" See some papers in *One in Christ*, vol. 12, nos. 3 and 4 (1976).

decisions will be taken. There is a kind of living example taking place around us of how churches in their dividedness actually make doctrinal decisions. Let no one mistake the significance of what is taking place in that process.

To give one example: There appears to be some tension between denominational response-making and an ecumenical process of arriving at responses. It seems to me that the denominations have to make their own responses. They are the ones who, regrettably but really, in a divided Christianity have the powers of decision, and, therefore, responses must come from existing denominational structures. Yet, we have already started to move beyond that, and we realize that no church decides in isolation. That is where the ecumenical part of the response and reception comes in. It calls for discussion, however informally or formally, in ecumenical groups. Therefore each denomination, in making its response, will already have listened in part to what some of its neighbors are saying in making their responses, and each decision will be partly affected, one would hope and pray, by what the neighbors are doing. So, it may well be that we are feeling our way toward a process by which the denominations, as long as they continue to exist, will gradually take more and more account of what other denominations are doing in their decision-making processes, until (please God) the day arrives when the churches can actually abandon their separating structures and make decisions together.

2. *The proclamation of BEM—a chance for the church.* From that living illustration of how churches at present decide with authority on matters of doctrine, we are building up, we hope, to the time when BEM or something close to it can be authoritatively proclaimed by the church as a whole. We may be working through processes that lead to what some hope for as a "genuinely ecumenical council."[8] When the denominational churches would have come so close together that they were able to recognize the Christian faith in each other, then a council could be convened with a recognition that it was already a council of unity-in-the-making; that council would then take the risk of making an authoritative dogmatic statement together. That would be an exercise in churchly unity and would itself be one instance of a genuinely united church. That is the way we are moving. We are being led from convergence to consensus. At the moment we are converging from very different starting points and are moving toward consensus which, when it is there, can be authoritatively proclaimed by an organ of the united church of Jesus Christ.

C. The Contemporary Confession of the Apostolic Faith

1. *Methods.* BEM gives us an example, first, of the methods of determining what the Apostolic Faith is. BEM could not have been produced without the

---

[8]See L. Vischer, "'A Genuinely Universal Council . . .'?" in *Ecumenical Review* 22 (1970): 97-106.

achievement of the Montreal World Conference in 1963, concerning Scripture, Tradition, and traditions. The big distinction was made between Scripture and Tradition on the one hand, and particular traditions on the other, and a working agreement was achieved whereby it was recognized that there is only one gospel, that the great Tradition is the transmission of that gospel through time, and that its primary and normative witness in the Scriptures shapes in both content and form what the church believes. BEM is an attempt to go to the Scriptures, as they live in the understanding and practice of the churches and the church, in order to discern the Apostolic Faith in whose light particular traditions have to be interpreted and, where necessary, corrected. BEM is a test for the legitimacy of going to what *a* church and *the* church actually say and do in their worship and communal life, in order to know what *a* church and *the* church believe; and, if this method of operation is established in connection with BEM, it will also become important for the Apostolic Faith study. To put it the other way around: study of the historical *effects* of Scripture, both in their controversial and in their unitive aspects, is becoming part of the exegesis of the Scriptures as an ecclesial book. If Scripture is to retain its normative status and function, the search will be for the beginnings, in the Scriptures, of what New Testament scholars have taught us to call "trajectories" which lead from the Bible into continuing church life.[9]

2. *Contexts.* We come, second, to the context for explicating the Apostolic Faith—what at our Rome meeting we called the hermeneutical aspect of our task. BEM indicates that at least one context for explicating the Apostolic Faith is the worship and sacramental life of the church: baptism, eucharist, and ministry. That is important, because it safeguards the doxological intention of all confession of faith. We are not confessing primarily for our own benefit or even for the benefit of the world. We are confessing to give glory to God, and that anchorage in the liturgical life of the church sets the prime context for our explicating the Apostolic Faith.

Then, too, BEM takes the question of context in the broader sense of contextualization—the relation of the confession of the faith to different cultures, different historical moments, different circumstances, and different issues. In the worship life of the church these things have very often found a home. Worship has somehow made the congregation a place in which people feel at home, and, therefore, the issues of their times and cultures find their way with them into the liturgical life of the church. When we are looking at how to confess the Apostolic Faith today, we have to look at how the churches are related to their contexts in the broader sense of culture, historical moment, and so on. That method was to some extent followed in the study which produced the Bangalore declaration on hope, which was enthusiastically received but will not itself be

---

[9]See the volumes edited by R. E. Brown et al., *Peter in the New Testament* (Minneapolis: Augsburg, 1973), and *Mary in the New Testament* (Philadelphia: Fortress, 1978).

the textual basis of a confessional dogmatic agreement. It is not that kind of document.[10] But this study at least helped to show how we could integrate materials which people were singing in Latin America and praying in Asia, how we could find expressed in them a common hope. That is promising for the discernment of a common faith also, and for a simultaneous recognition of both its culturally conditioned expressions and their power to speak cross-culturally.[11]

3. *Forms.* Finally, BEM shows us the forms, or some of the forms, in which the Apostolic Faith is and can be confessed today. That is part of what the Rome report called the constructive task of the Apostolic Faith study: to find the means and forms by which we can together make common confession of faith. BEM shows us that there are at least three forms in which we can do this, and they have to do with baptism, eucharist, and ministry. The very act of coming and asking for baptism and being baptized is a confession of faith. The rite is accompanied by words. The act itself and the words that are said there are one form of confessing the Apostolic Faith together, so it matters what questions are put to the candidates, what responses they make, and what words the minister says in baptizing.

In the eucharist, too, the very act of assembling around the communion table is a form of confessing the Apostolic Faith. "As often as you eat this bread and drink this cup, you proclaim the Lord's death until he comes." The assembling and the act of eating and drinking are already a confession, and the words said over the bread and wine state in verbal form the Apostolic Faith. It therefore matters what content we put into that central prayer of the church, the great eucharistic prayer.

As to ministry, the very way a church shapes its internal life and its ministry of evangelism and service in the world is itself an act of confessing. The sheer sociological shape of ministry speaks: who does what, and how, and when, among ordained ministers in their different orders, if there are more than one, and among laypeople with their different gifts, and how the two are related, and so on. And it obviously matters, too, what faith it is that a bishop is ordained to safeguard and transmit, what faith it is that a presbyter is ordained to preach, and so on.

BEM, then, points to baptism, eucharist, and the ministry of the church as forms of the confession of the Apostolic Faith today. It is here that revision of our liturgical rites and reform of our ministerial patterns come in. The Preface to BEM asks the churches to state "the extent to which your church can recog-

---

[10]"A Common Account of Hope" was published in *Commission on Faith and Order, Bangalore, 1978: Sharing in One Hope*, Faith and Order Paper 92 (Geneva: World Council of Churches, 1978), pp. 1-11.
[11]Already the Lausanne Conference of 1927 declared: "We believe that the Holy Spirit in leading the Church into all truth may enable it, while firmly adhering to the witness of these Creeds (our common heritage from the ancient Church), to *express the truths of revelation in such other forms as new problems may from time to time demand.*"

nize in this text the faith of the Church through the ages." That does not mean simply testing BEM for its accord with "what we, in our particular traditions, have always said and done." That is part of it, for we have received blessings even in our separation, but each church must also be willing to revise and reform its rites and practices in light of an ecumenical reading of Scripture and Tradition. That is why the Preface to BEM also invites the churches to decide on "the guidance your church can take from this text for its worship, educational, ethical, and spiritual life and witness." There is not a single denominational church whose present life escapes critical questioning from some of the paragraphs of BEM.

With a look to common constructive work for the future, we may note the interesting phenomenon of the so-called Lima Liturgy. This eucharistic rite was originally composed for celebration at the Lima meeting of Faith and Order, and it was later used in revised form at the Vancouver Assembly of the W.C.C. It was intended simply as *one* "liturgical expression of convergence in faith achieved in Baptism, Eucharist and Ministry." But the enthusiasm with which it is being taken into local use in many places suggests that, despite the oft-repeated assurance which ecumenical leaders feel compelled to give that unity does not mean uniformity, there exists among Christians a real eagerness to have a rite and text which, at least in occasional use, allows them to confess their faith together in eucharistic mode.

III. Conclusion

The complex relations between BEM and the Apostolic Faith study have been outlined. An opportunity for seeing how they are running together will be given by the next World Conference on Faith and Order, which is being projected for 1987 or 1988. It must be remembered that the W.C.C. has instructed Faith and Order to resume a study on which it has proved particularly difficult to get a grip hitherto: "The Unity of the Church and the Renewal of Human Community." That is the most eschatological of themes, and it provides the widest context for both BEM and the Apostolic Faith. It may be that our global and threatened epoch will lend a sense of urgency to the task.[12] It is only as the church realizes "visible unity in one faith and in one eucharistic fellowship" that the church can truly be what Vatican II called it: "a sign and instrument of communion with God and of unity among all people."

---

[12]G. Wainwright, *The Ecumenical Moment*, in particular, chap. 1.

BEM AND THE COMMUNITY OF WOMEN AND MEN

Francine Cardman

Longer ago than we might like to remember, Virginia Woolf observed and analyzed a phenomenon which says worlds about the significance of our topic: the community of women and men and the reception by the churches of the *Baptism, Eucharist, and Ministry* document (hereafter, BEM). In *Three Guineas* she astutely and archly demonstrated the way in which three causes—the education of women, the advancement of women's professional employment, and the effort to end war—were really "inseparable and the same." At the end of her reflection she concluded that she should donate a guinea to each cause: "a free gift, given freely, without any other conditions than you choose to impose upon yourself."[1] Like Virginia Woolf, women and men in the church are coming to the realization that the search for the unity of the church and the struggle for the liberation of women have much in common, mutually influencing each other for good or for ill and, in the process, advancing or setting back the cause of human peace and wholeness, of shalom. Unlike the money donated by Woolf to her three causes, the wholeness we seek has been ours from the beginning, a gift freely given, but squandered by the conditions we have imposed upon it, so now we must seek the gift anew, asking not only the original Giver, but also, in all humility, one another. What we seek and how we seek it are thus the subjects of these reflections on BEM and the community of women and men.

As the Preface to BEM notes, the ecumenical movement seems to be at a moment of *kairos*.[2] Both the document itself and the process of its reception represent a crucial point in the search for the visible unity of the church. I want to suggest that the *kairos* quality of the moment has much to do with the *way* in which we go about seeking reception and consensus. This time of choice has as much to do with the sort of community that is seeking unity as it does with the sort of unity that is sought. In particular, it has to do with the participation

---

[1]Virginia Woolf, *Three Guineas* (1938; reprinted: New York: Harcourt Brace Jovanovich, 1966), p. 144.

[2]*Baptism, Eucharist, and Ministry*, Faith and Order Paper 111 (Geneva: World Council of Churches, 1982), p. x.

Francine Cardman (Roman Catholic) is Associate Professor of Historical Theology at Weston School of Theology, Cambridge, MA. She has a B.A. from Swarthmore College and an M.Phil. and Ph.D. (1974) from Yale University. President of the North American Academy of Ecumenists for 1980-82, she has been a member of the Eastern Orthodox-Roman Catholic Consultation since late-1982. Recently published articles include "Cyprian and Rome: The Controversy over Baptism," in H. Küng and J. Moltmann, eds., *The Right to Dissent*, Concilium 158 (Seabury, 1982), and " 'The Church Would Look Foolish without Them': Women and Laity since Vatican II," in Gerald M. Fagin, ed., *Vatican II: Open Questions and New Horizons* (Michael Glazier, 1984).

83

of and attentiveness to women—and, thereby, to the possibility of a community of women and men—in the process of reception of BEM.

That this should be so is due, I think, to the fact that the ecumenical movement and the women's movement share concerns and goals that are essentially similar, if not finally the same. Ecumenism has a dual focus: it is concerned with fostering unity and community within and among the Christian churches, and it does so in and for a broken world. The women's movement, too, has a dual focus: it is a movement for the liberation and wholeness of women, and it looks, ultimately, for the unity and community of humankind, women and men. The women's movement must be understood in the context of other movements for liberation throughout the world, just as the ecumenical movement must be seen in the light of struggles for a just and peaceful human community. The goals of both movements might be summed up in this fashion: the creation of an inclusive human community, extending to all aspects of life, in which the full possibilities of each person and all peoples can be realized in harmony and mutuality. The hope in this vision is the hope of the reconciliation of "all things" as acclaimed in the great hymn of cosmic redemption in the first chapter of Colossians.

It is from this angle of vision, then, that I want to explore some of the ways in which the concerns of BEM intersect with the human hope for shalom, for a community of women and men in the church and beyond it. I begin by asking further about the connections between the BEM project and the Community study.[3] Then I will put the question of connections to each section of BEM, with considerably more attention to the ministry section than to those on baptism or eucharist. I conclude with some reflections on possible future lines of development, not only in the reception process, but also in the ongoing programs and studies of Faith and Order.

Connections between the Studies

Sexism is sin and leads to division. The myth of female inferiority distorts the faith and corrupts the order of the church. . . . When the question is raised and examined, therefore, of a new community of women and men in the church, we are not dealing merely with one problem area among many others. What is at stake is the achievement of the one church of Jesus Christ and also the full humanity of the human being, whether male or female.[4]

---

[3]The report on the conference which concluded the Community study is published in Constance Parvey, ed., *The Community of Women and Men in the Church: The Sheffield Report* (Geneva: W.C.C., 1983). Some additional addresses and papers from Sheffield can be found in *Mid-Stream*, vol. 21, no. 3 (July, 1982).

[4]Lazareth's remarks are quoted by Christa Springe, "Learning from Sheffield," *Ecumenical Review* 34 (1982): 169.

This stark analysis is William Lazareth's, offered at the 1981 Sheffield conference. Despite its clarity, and despite almost sixty years of sporadic attention to so-called "women's concerns" by the World Council of Churches, the full impact of the hope for new community has yet to make itself felt on the classical agenda of Faith and Order. One of the most significant things to notice about both BEM and the beginnings of the reception process is the remarkable lack of attention to either the Community study or women's concerns. Requests and recommendations from the Community study were duly received and duly noted at Bangalore in 1978, and in 1982 at Lima, for instance, but one must strain to see their influence on the BEM document or the reception process thus far.[5]

True, more inclusive language has made an appearance in the text, especially in the baptism and eucharist sections. (The language of the ministry section is so studiously genderless in regard to the person of the minister that I take this to be not so much an exercise in inclusive language as an exercise in avoidance.) It is also true that there are some explicit questions about the ministry of women in the study guide to BEM,[6] and that the Preface to the document itself notes the importance of the "widest possible involvement of the whole people of God" in the process of receiving the text.[7] But it is also and more importantly true that almost no correlations are made in any of the sections of BEM with the insights and issues raised up by the Community study. Likewise, only the scantest attention is paid, in either the text or the commentary, to the most obvious point of present and potential disagreement, namely, the ordination of women. Because there is also no explicit correlation among the sections of BEM, themes and approaches in the first two sections which might prove helpful in confronting this delicately sidestepped crux fail to be exploited, or even noticed.

---

[5]For Bangalore, see in *Sharing in One Hope, Reports and Documents from the Meeting of Faith and Order Commission, Bangalore, 1978*, Faith and Order Paper 92 (Geneva: W.C.C., n.d.): "Towards Fuller Community of Women and Men in the Church," with recommendations on pp. 163-164, and "The Unity of the Church and the Community of Women and Men in the Church," with recommendations on pp. 269-270. For Lima, see Michael Kinnamon, ed., *Towards Visible Unity, Commission of Faith and Order, Lima, 1982*, Faith and Order Paper 112 (Geneva: W.C.C., 1982), vol. 1, report on plenary session on Community study, pp. 126-130; vol. 2, "The Community Study and Apostolic Faith . . .," pp. 47-50, and "The Community Study and the Unity of the Church and the Renewal of Human Community," by Mary Tanner, pp. 153-165. It is instructive, e.g., to notice the outcome of the recommendation made by the Community study at Lima, that "the volume of theological essays on the BEM text should include one or two essays on the theme, especially as it relates to the ordination of women to diaconal and eucharistic ministries" (p. 129). There is *no* essay in Max Thurian, ed., *Ecumenical Perspectives on Baptism, Eucharist, and Ministry*, Faith and Order Paper 116 (Geneva: W.C.C., 1983), which treats the Community study and its implications for BEM. Of the two essays on ministry, Emmanuel Lanne's "Convergence on the Ordained Ministry" simply mentions that BEM did not "tackle" the question of women's ordination, then goes on to discuss its positive contributions, while Geoffrey Wainwright's "Reconciliation in Ministry" does not mention it at all.

[6]William H. Lazareth, *Growing Together in Baptism, Eucharist, and Ministry: A Study Guide*, Faith and Order Paper 114 (Geneva: W.C.C., 1982).

[7]*Baptism, Eucharist, and Ministry*, p. x.

One of the reasons for the lack of engagement between the Community study and BEM has to do with the difference of method between the two projects. Although BEM's language and impetus are sometimes contextual, it more often locates its concerns in the classical controversies and historical divisions of the churches, as the Preface acknowledges. As a result, BEM frequently appears overly preoccupied with the concerns of the religious professionals—clergy, hierarchs, theologians—rather than those of the diverse people of God as a whole. One wonders what might have happened had BEM engaged in a grassroots, contextual process of reflection and revision *before* Lima rather than waiting until a final text had been formulated and the process of reception begun in order to solicit that kind of participation and response.

The question of method points to a second possible reason for the curious lack of engagement between BEM and the Community study: the discomfort produced by newer modes of theological reflection—such as feminist theology or liberation theology—so that they are often perceived, in Letty Russell's words, "as so much of a threat to the theological and ecclesiastical establishment that what is said is dismissed as inadequate or disruptive to the search for unity."[8] The challenge that such theologies present to classical ecumenical method was not faced in the BEM process, despite the period of response and revision that followed the Accra version of the text. In good measure because it was not, it remains to be met on the even more volatile issue of women's ordination.

But critique should not be mistaken for ingratitude. It precedes the quest for future directions toward unity on this and other issues which might lie dormant in the text of BEM itself. So it is important to ask what "hints half-guessed" there might be in the gifts offered by BEM, even if they are not all the gifts one might have hoped for at this time.

Baptism

Two questions can profitably be put to the section on baptism: what kind of community and what kind of Christ is baptism about? BEM speaks eloquently about baptism as incorporation into the new community and liberation into the new humanity. It understands the new life of baptism to be a sign of the reign of God, and baptized believers as persons capable of demonstrating that humanity can be regenerated and liberated (2, 6, 7, 10). Only once does it mention the reality of continued divisions in this new community (6). In the commentary, race, sex, and social status are simply noted as divisions which can call into question the baptismal unity of the Christian community. By considering the

---

[8]Letty M. Russell, "Ecumenical Implications of Feminist Theologies," *Ecumenical Trends* 11 (1982): 137. The methodological disparity is a major factor, I think, in accounting for Faith and Order's inability to integrate the findings of the "Giving Account of Hope" study, beyond having produced the statement, "A Common Account of Hope" at Bangalore (see *Sharing in One Hope*).

sign value of the life of the baptized community more fully, it might be possible to come to a deeper understanding of the gravity of the countersign raised by the continuation and legitimation of inequality and division in the church on the basis of race, sex, or class. Or, as the Bangalore report, "Towards a Fuller Community of Women and Men in the Church," put it:

> Many of us felt that the Church should not reflect all the brokenness of the society, and that by perpetuating the same evils of caste, class and the oppression of the weaker sections of society, the Church was making a mockery of the Gospel message and its calling to the ministry of reconciliation.[9]

The kind of community implied by the baptism section, then, would be a community of equals, signed with a common discipleship, and sharing the fruits of the Spirit in the fullness of its life together.

What kind of Christ is imaged in and by the community brought into being through baptism? BEM envisions baptism as the basic bond of unity which enables Christians to be witnesses to the healing and reconciling love of God. This baptismal unity also calls the churches "to overcome their divisions and visibly manifest their fellowship" for the sake of that witness (6). It would be helpful, therefore, to reflect further on the significance of baptism as a call to ministry, a call to share in and continue Jesus' ministry of reconciling and redemptive love. The call is addressed not only to the community as a whole but also to each member of it. Thus, all are called to grow to the measure of the fullness of the stature of Christ. All are called to represent Christ in a real and significant way, to each other in the community, and to all others in the world. By virtue of having "put on" Christ, every baptized believer, female as well as male, has the sacramental capacity to represent both Christ and the community—for they have become that body which is the presence of Christ in the world today.[10] If the realistic sense of the sign value of life in the community of the baptized were more fully developed in this fashion, the connections to the community of women and men would become clearer and the imperatives for a renewed life more obvious.

Finally, I simply want to observe here that there is something of a time-bomb—not exactly a pleasant "gift"—in the text's lack of attention to the male language of the trinitarian baptismal formula and the difficulties this is already raising for some women and even a few men in the church.[11]

---

[9]*Sharing in One Hope*, p. 158.
[10]Elizabeth Bettenhausen characterizes the ecclesiology implied in this description as a "baptismal ecclesiology" and contrasts it with an "episcopal ecclesiology" which views the church as best represented by its ordained ministries, especially bishops, in "Women and Youth at Vancouver," in *Mid-Stream* 23 (January, 1984): 93, 99-100.
[11]I am not suggesting that the traditional trinitarian formula ought to be discarded, but simply that the problem presented by its male language ought to be recognized, and that additional, nonsexist formulas are needed to supplement the traditional usage on at least *some* of the occasions in which the Trinity is named in the context of the church's worship.

Eucharist

The issues of Christ and community are as significant for eucharist as they are for baptism. Within the remarkably rich understanding of eucharist presented by BEM, questions about the quality of the *koinonia* and the clarity of the Christ imaged in and by the community need to be faced more directly than they are in the text. In regard to the nature of the community, there are important hints in the way the text describes the gathering of Christians for eucharist. They become one people (26); they receive the gift of salvation (6); they enter into communion with Christ and with the body of Christ which is the church (19). The fullness of the eucharistic community embraces all aspects of life, demanding reconciliation and sharing (20). Thus, through communion in Jesus Christ, every Christian—female as well as male—is renewed again and again (6) and gradually transformed into the image of Christ (26). This sense of the divinization which flows from eucharist has profound possibilities for opening our understanding of who may image Christ in the community. In turn, it can also help us to see how this openness to the transforming power of the eucharist is grounded in the grace of baptism, by which a person takes on the identity of the community, and its life becomes their own.

It is surprising, therefore, that the eucharist section does not take up the crucial question of the representation of Christ. Who may represent Christ and how this representation is made possible are not addressed directly in the text. Because of their importance for questions of ministry, this lack is regrettable. The discussion of the transformative nature of eucharist, however, offers some suggestions for further development, as does the emphatic assertion, "It is Christ who invites to the meal and who presides at it" (29). However, the identification of the minister of the eucharist as "the ambassador who represents the divine initiative" (29) is replete with difficulties which are not even noted in the commentary.[12] Yet, by not specifying the one who presides at the eucharist, except to observe that "in most churches this presidency is signified by an ordained minister" (29), the text may be leaving matters open for future determination as the church's understanding and practice of ministry continue to evolve.

Ministry

A deepening appreciation of the ministry of the whole people of God may be one source for such continued growth. Although BEM intends to ground the

---

[12]Of particular importance is the way in which "divine initiative" has often been understood as a generative, hence *male*, activity. Aside from the question of whether anyone can represent God's initiative, it is necessary to ask how the eucharistic minister differs in this regard from any other baptized Christian. Geoffrey Wainwright attempted a brief exegesis of the notion of representation in his essay, "Reconciliation in Ministry," p. 135, but this goes beyond the text.

ordained ministry in the ministry of the whole church, the very lopsidedness of the text makes this effort problematic.[13] It also makes it possible that, by concentrating on historic questions of faith and order, the entire ministry section may be misplacing its attention and, thereby, missing the real ferment in ministry today and the promise it holds for the future. Further reflection on the significance of the ministry of the whole church and of all Christians as a serious locus of real ministry is thus necessary. When we consider that all Christians, women and men alike, are called to ministry and mission in some way and at some time, it may make it possible for us to relate ordained ministry and sacraments to the social mission of the church. It is also possible that such reflection may help overcome the breach between clergy and laity which is maintained by even as benign an understanding of the ordained ministry as that presented in BEM. If this gap could be bridged, it might also relieve some of the pressure of the double bind in which women find themselves in those churches where ordination is restricted to men and where women are always numbered among the laity. Attending to the sociological consequences of faith and practice, therefore, is as important in regard to ministry as it is to baptism and eucharist, for the quality of the community's life together and the clarity of the image of Christ it embodies are directly affected by the way in which it welcomes and orders the charisms of its members and, thereby, ministers in Christ's name.

In light of the suggestions from this section and the previous ones on baptism and eucharist, it is, perhaps, now possible to address the issue of the ordination of women with a somewhat lowered level of anxiety and a fuller hope for the unity of the church.

BEM and the Ordination of Women

Probably the most notable point about BEM's treatment of the ordination of women is its brevity. In comparison with earlier W.C.C. studies and statements on ministry, as well as with the Accra version of the text, BEM has considerably reduced its estimate of the significance of this question for the recognition and reconciliation of ministries.[14] Not only has the number of lines of text devoted to the matter dropped sharply from previous discussions, but the force-

---

[13]The six opening paragraphs on "The Calling of the Whole People of God" are a marked improvement from earlier texts and drafts, but its failure to influence significantly the tone and direction of the major portion of the ministry section is most evident when compared with the presentation of ministry in the revised chapter 7 of *In Quest of a Church of Christ Uniting*, rev. (Princeton: Consultation on Church Union, 1980).

[14]The major documents which have contributed to the evolution of the ministry section include: "The Ordained Ministry," in "On the Way to Communion in the Sacraments," *Louvain 1971*, Faith and Order Paper 59 (Geneva: W.C.C., 1971), pp. 78-101; the draft prepared at the Marseilles consultation on the ordained ministry in 1972, "The Ordained Ministry in Ecumenical Perspective," SE/34, *Study Encounter*, vol. 8, no. 4 (1972), pp. 1-21; and the text approved at Accra in 1974, and authorized for distribution at the Nairobi

fulness with which it is addressed has also diminished. Consider, for instance, the following quotations from Accra and BEM respectively:

Accra, 1974

(64) Both men and women need to discover the full meaning of their specific contribution to the ministry of Christ. The Church is entitled to the style of ministry which can be provided by women as well as that which can be provided by men. Indeed, an understanding of our mutual interdependence needs to be more widely reflected in all branches of ministry. . . .

(65) Since those who advocate the ordination of women do so out of their understanding of the meaning of the Gospel and ordination, and since the experience of the churches in which women are ordained has on the whole been positive and none has found reason to reconsider its decision, the question must be asked as to whether it is not time for all the churches to confront this matter forthrightly.[15]

BEM, 1982

[Ministry] (18) Both women and men must discover together their contributions to the service of Christ in the Church. The Church must discover the ministry which can be provided by women as well as that which can be provided by men. A deeper understanding of the comprehensiveness of ministry which reflects the interdependence of men and women needs to be more widely manifested in the life of the Church.

Though they agree on this need, the churches draw different conclusions as to the admission of women to the ordained ministry.[16]

A look at the history of the discussion of women's ordination in W.C.C. circles makes BEM's cautious retreat on the topic all the more problematic. As early as New Delhi, the question of the ordination of women had received attention. Then the Department of Faith and Order was requested to organize a study on the topic, in conjunction with the Department on Cooperation of Men and Women in Church, Family, and Society. Since that 1963 consultation and the Faith and Order Conference at Montreal later that year, the subject has continued to haunt the faith and order agenda.[17] It arose at consultations in 1970 (Cartigny) and 1979 (Klingenthal); it found its way to Faith and Order meetings

---

Assembly in 1975, "The Ministry," in *One Baptism, One Eucharist, and a Mutually Recognized Ministry*, Faith and Order Paper 73 (Geneva: W.C.C., 1975), pp. 29-56.

[15]*One Baptism . . .*, p. 45.

[16]*Baptism, Eucharist, and Ministry*, p. 24.

[17]*Concerning the Ordination of Women* (Geneva: W.C.C., 1964) is the report from the consultation; the report of Section II at Montreal, "The Redemptive Work of Christ and the Ministry of His Church," is contained in P. C. Rodger and L. Vischer, eds., *The Fourth World Conference on Faith and Order, the Report from Montreal, 1963* (New York: Association Press, 1964).

at Louvain (1971), Marseilles (1972), Accra (1974), and, eventually, by way of Crêt Barard (1977), to Sheffield (1981), Lima (1982), and Vancouver (1983).[18] Some of the ghost's appearances occur in the ambit of BEM, others in the context of the Community study—and it is around to haunt us still. Given its history and its evident health in the present, it is beside the point to ask whether and how serious an ecumenical and theological question the ordination of women is. It is, however, meaningful to ask whether there can be recognition and reconciliation of ministries without agreement on this matter. In terms of BEM, this translates into two distinct questions: what does the issue of women's ordination mean for reception *by the churches*? and what does it mean in terms of reception *by women*? It is important to note that the two are not coextensive.

In order to answer these questions, it is necessary to go back to more of the history of the text before going forward to its possible future. The argument from experience—in this case, the positive experience of those churches which ordain women—figured prominently in the texts from Louvain, Marseilles, and Accra, but it dropped out of the text of BEM and was relegated to a note in the commentary. The same thing happened to the acknowledgement that for many the matter is a question of the meaning of the gospel, as was noted in the three earlier texts. The Accra statement offered the strongest treatment of the subject, but, despite the fact that a minority of replies received and reviewed at Crêt Barard were negative toward the ordination of women, its treatment in the Lima text was substantially reduced, and the significance attached to it was considerably less than the prior discussion would have suggested that it merited.[19] Here, more than anywhere else, BEM seems to be either out of touch with the Community study or else unwilling to grapple with the issues it raises. In BEM the facing of conflict fades before the hope of concord, but conflict concealed is conflict nevertheless, and it will in time be revealed as such. In 1971 at Louvain the issue was already past due: "This question must be faced, and the time to face it is now." We can be sure that its ghost will again rise up to haunt us.

Before it does, we would do well to ask whether the BEM text itself suggests some approaches and perspectives which might help move us toward resolution. There are several. The most important is the positive regard given to the diversity

---

[18]Cartigny report: Brigalia Bam, ed., *What Is Ordination Coming To?* (Geneva: W.C.C., 1971). The Klingenthal consultation resulted in a "workbook" rather than a report as such: Constance Parvey, ed., *Ordination of Women in Ecumenical Perspective: Workbook for the Church's Future*, Faith and Order Paper 105 (Geneva: W.C.C., 1980). Responses to the Accra text were the subject of the Crêt Barard consultation, reported in *Towards an Ecumenical Consensus: Baptism, Eucharist, Ministry*, Faith and Order Paper 84 (Geneva: W.C.C., 1977). See n. 17, above, for other studies and reports relating to ordination. The topic appears several times in the Vancouver report, *Gathered for Life: Official Report, VI Assembly, World Council of Churches, Vancouver, Canada, 24 July-10August, 1983*. Edited by David Gill (Geneva: W.C.C.; Grand Rapids: Eerdmans, 1983), pp. 58, 68; cf. pp. 49-50 on BEM and the Community study.

[19]*Towards an Ecumenical Consensus*, p. 17.

of gifts and charisms in the community (3, 5, 23, 32). If this insight were related more integrally to the text's understanding of priesthood, and especially to the relation between the priesthood of all the baptized and that of the ordained minister, then perhaps it would be possible to reach some consensus on who may exercise the charism of ministry in the church. Likewise, the text's insistence that authority in the community is not a personal possession might also make it possible in time not to have to draw attention to the gender of the person who exercises that authority. Another promising direction is one which seemed to emerge at Marseilles, only to disappear again: namely, the suggestion that the ordination of women may be a matter of church discipline rather than of doctrine:

> For most communions, the role of women in the ministry is a matter of discipline and not of doctrine, although there are doctrinal positions relevant to the question. If agreement could be reached that the disciplinary status of the question predominates, the issue could be decided by a future ecumenical council.[20]

The disciplinary aspects of the question are suggested at various points in the BEM text (6, 27, 49) and, with further attention, could acquire more definite features in the future.

In the meantime, it is necessary to keep pursuing the question of whether disagreement on the subject constitutes an insurmountable obstacle to the recognition and reconciliation of ministries. A "yes" can arise from at least two directions: from the Roman Catholic, Orthodox, and those evangelical churches which do not ordain women, on the ground of either normative tradition or scriptural mandate; or it may come from those women and men who hold that the question touches the heart of the gospel and the very nature of the church. I must confess that I find myself among the latter group. At the same time, because it *is* such a central and critical question, I do not think that it can be resolved by either hasty consensus or refusal of dialogue. Rather, I am hopeful that, in the very effort to explicate the questions and explore the dimensions of the conflict, we will find a way to grow together toward agreement.

Thus, the churches are called to confess their division on this matter and to seek together the way which will lead to reconciliation. A major step along that way would be the participation of women from all parts of the church in the BEM reception process as dialogue partners whose insights and issues are acknowledged as crucial for any real progress. As long as women are missing from this process, the churches will be prevented from reaching any lasting agreement. How, then, might we begin to move toward reception and consensus?

---

[20]"The Ordained Ministry in Ecumenical Perspective," p. 13.

Reflections for the Future

I can offer neither map nor detailed directions, but I can point to some paths which seem more promising than others.

First, we must continue to pay attention to and make possible the full participation of women in the process of reception. Not since the Empress Pulcheria moved the church to Chalcedonian orthodoxy by her adamant nonreception of the "robber council" of Ephesus in 449; not since the Empress Irene ensured the restoration of the icons and the "triumph of Orthodoxy" in 843, through her insistent reception of Nicaea II; not, that is, since the last of the great councils of the so-called undivided church have women had such a role to play in any process of reception, conciliar or otherwise.

Second, continued dialogue with the Community study and with the responses, recommendations, and concerns which have arisen from it is a necessity, not only in regard to the reception of BEM, but also in carrying out such current Faith and Order projects as that "Towards a Common Confession of the Apostolic Faith" and the effort on "The Unity of the Church and Renewal of the Human Community."[21] Among the worldwide contributions to the Community study, for instance, the statement on "Authority-in-Community" from the National Council of Churches of Christ stands out as deserving of far more attention than it has received, even among the N.C.C.C.'s own constituency.[22] In regard to the Apostolic Faith project, the thoughtful reflections presented at Lima by the Community working group require careful consideration, since the concerns raised touch on every item of the Creed, compelling us to ask about the kind of community in which it is confessed, "is it possible for the community of women and men . . . to accept the Creed?"[23] Similarly, the aim of relating the goal of ecumenism—the unity of the church—to the renewal of the human community cannot be realized without seriously confronting the obstacles to both unity and community presented by the systematic subordination of women in the church and beyond it. These three projects—BEM, the Apostolic Faith, and Renewal of Human Community—will remain abstract exercises unless they can attend to the fundamental questions that hinder or foster the formation of community between women and men.

Third, the doctrinal and scriptural questions about the ordination of women must be faced squarely, both within the churches and, as BEM acknowledges, among the churches, in joint study and discussion. Among the more important topics which bear on the matter are these: Christology (which might especially benefit from a careful look at the Chalcedonian definition and the controversies that preceded it), theological anthropology (of which I will say more below), the

---

[21]See the report from Lima, *Towards Visible Unity*, vol. 1, Sections V and VII.

[22]Authority-in-Community," drafted by Madeleine Boucher, *Mid-Stream* 21 (1982): 402-417.

[23]*Towards Visible Unity*, vol. 2, p. 48.

authority and interpretation of Scripture, the authority and interpretation of tradition, and the language and imagery of the Trinity, or what Sallie McFague terms "metaphorical theology."[24]

Fourth, and finally, I want to suggest that it may be time to refocus the ecumenical discussion about the ordination of women. Rather than the Roman Catholic and Orthodox churches' continuing to regard the ordination of women by many Protestant churches as further evidence for their lurking suspicions about the legitimacy or reality of Protestant orders and sacraments, it might now be time for these churches—and those Anglican bodies that do not yet ordain women—to consider seriously the closer ties and steps toward unity with the churches of the Reformation which might be achieved by ordaining women to sacramental ministry and priesthood. For conservative evangelical churches, too, the time may have come to reconsider the way they read the Scriptures and to ask what can be learned from dialogue with other Protestant churches which hear the word of God differently. Perhaps it is time, too, to shift at least some of the burden of responsibility in this matter. Why should the onus of continuing ecclesial division rest solely on those churches that ordain women, rather than being shared humbly and equally by those that do not? It is just possible, given God's will for the unity of the church and of the human community, that out of our efforts to hear and respond faithfully and freely to the questions raised by women's ordination the churches will come to know the nature and extent of both unity and diversity.

Until the burden is shifted and shared, and as long as the disjunction between the women's movement and the ecumenical movement remains a reality of our practice, if not of our rhetoric, neither the unity of the church nor the renewal of the human community will be a real possibility. Until the day when "women's concerns" become integral to the project of realizing the new community of women and men, in the church and beyond the church, we will continue to squander our gifts in the same way that those who benefited from Virginia Woolf's three guineas have squandered theirs from that day until this. Until then, we may be able to make a common confession, but it will not be the faith called into being by the gospel of Jesus Christ. Until then, we may strive to renew the human community, but we will be a sign of contradiction rather than a sign of hope. For we will not yet have grappled with the most basic question of all: the full humanity of both women and men, so reconciled and so transformed in Christ that they both represent Christ in and through the Christian community, for each other and for the whole of humankind.

In the end, then, it is probably the question of anthropology on which the whole matter rests. For it comes down, really, to this: are women human? A corollary question must also be asked: are women Christian? And, if the possibility of receiving and exercising the charism of ordained ministry does not

---

[24]Sallie McFague, *Metaphorical Theology: Models of God in Religious Language* (Philadelphia: Fortress Press, 1982).

extend to women, this deficiency of baptismal grace will force us to ask the most basic question of all: are women saved?

In her own idiosyncratic and now somewhat dated manner, another English woman of letters, Dorothy Sayers, asked just that in her 1941 essay, "The Human-Not-Quite-Human." Forced to conclude, on the basis of their treatment in church and society, that "women are not human," she wryly remarked that "God, of course, may have His own opinion, but the Church is reluctant to endorse it." She ended her observations by commenting on the contrast between the unique way in which Jesus related to women and the all-too-predictable behavior of his followers then and now. Her reflections are a fitting conclusion to this discussion of women and men in the church as well:

> Perhaps it is no wonder that the women were first at the Cradle and last at the Cross. They had never known a man like this Man—there never has been such another. A prophet and teacher who never nagged at them, never flattered or coaxed or patronised; who never made arch jokes about them, never treated them either as "The women, God help us!" or "The ladies, God bless them!"; who rebuked without querulousness and praised without condescension; who took their questions and arguments seriously; who never mapped out their sphere for them, never urged them to be feminine or jeered at them for being female; who had no axe to grind and no uneasy male dignity to defend; who took them as he found them and was completely unself-conscious. There is no act, no sermon, no parable in the whole Gospel that borrows its pungency from female perversity; nobody could possibly guess from the words and deeds of Jesus that there was anything "funny" about woman's nature.

> But we might easily deduce it from His contemporaries, and from His prophets before Him, and from His Church to this day. Women are not human; nobody shall persuade that they are human; let them say what they like, we will not believe it, though One rose from the dead.[25]

---

[25]Reprinted in *Are Women Human?* (Grand Rapids: William B. Eerdmans, 1971), pp. 46-47.

BAPTISM, EUCHARIST, AND MINISTRY, RECEPTION, AND THE BILATERALS

David Willis

This essay offers four theses which are intended as part of the ongoing evaluation and reception of the *Baptism, Eucharist, and Ministry* (hereafter, BEM) document. These theses are, however, deliberately offered from a particular perspective, namely, that of seeing the process itself as an outworking, in the realization of a greater visible unity of the churches, of the Christian freedom which is the practice of justification and sanctification.[1]

I am aware that there is no single understanding of justification and sanctification agreed to by all participants. Yet, I am even more aware of the discernibly emerging clarification and even levels of agreement—if not yet a consensus—on that doctrine in bilateral conversations, and of the significant benefits of seeing the next steps as ones taken as expressions of the freedom of the Christian *anthropos* and church. A confessing stance is implied in this: at this particular juncture in the ecumenical movement, set as it is in the midst of a world which may technologically be drawn tighter, but which shows dreadful signs of cosmically destructive fragmentation and misuse of power, the churches seriously engaged in the ecumenical movement are in a *status confessionis*.

At stake, obviously, is not just the next chapter in the ecumenical movement or even the successful reception of a document at official levels, but what

---

[1]Cf. the deliberate use of the strong term "participation" in the life, death, and resurrection of Jesus Christ as the meaning of baptism (BEM, II, A), and the structure and wording in II, B: "Thus those baptized are pardoned, cleansed and sanctified by Christ and are given as part of their baptismal experience a new ethical orientation under the guidance of the Holy Spirit."

(Edward) David Willis (Presbyterian Church, U.S.A.) is Charles Hodge Professor of Systematic Theology at Princeton Theological Seminary and chair of the Theology Dept. He previously was on the faculty of San Francisco Theological Seminary and Graduate Theological Union, Berkeley, CA (1966-78), Princeton Theological Seminary (1963-66), and Harvard Divinity School (1961-63). He has also held short-term pastoral positions in Colorado, Pennsylvania, New England, and Switzerland. He holds a B.S. from Northwestern University, a B.D. from Princeton, and a Th.D. (1963) from Harvard Divinity School, with additional studies in Geneva and Berlin. Dr. Willis has been a member of the Reformed-Roman Catholic Consultation in America since 1972 and of the Theological Commission of the World Alliance of Reformed Churches since 1969. Long involved in numerous Presbyterian and ecumenical organizations and consultations, he was a member of the W.C.C. North American Committee on BEM, 1980-81, and participated in Reformed-Russian Orthodox dialogues in Leningrad and Budapest in 1976 and 1979. He edited *Pacific Theological Review* from 1974-78, and is on the editorial council of *Theology Today* and the editorial board of *Studies in the History of Christian Thought*, ed. H. Oberman (Brill, 1974——). His articles have appeared in a variety of journals over the last twenty years; most recent of his four books is *Daring Prayer* (John Knox, 1977). His "Confession: 9.5 Theses," appears in G. Békés and H. Meyer, eds., *Confession Fidei*, Studia Anselmiana 81 (Rome, 1982).

reception of this document implies in the commitment of churches as an effective sign of reconciliation in a torn world. The Barmen Declaration's strong language calls the church to a stance which applies analogously not only to the present political climate but also to the danger of exempting a portion of the churches' lives from Christ's claims. Put positively, "free, grateful service" is to characterize the very process in which we are engaged in considering the next step at this critical juncture of the ecumenical movement:

> As Jesus Christ is God's assurance of the forgiveness of all our sins, so in the same way and with the same seriousness he is also God's mighty claim upon our whole life. Through him befalls us a joyful deliverance from the godless fetters of this world for a free, grateful service to his creatures. We reject the false doctrine, as though there were areas of our life in which we would not belong to Jesus Christ, but to other lords—areas in which we would not need justification and sanctification through him.
>
> (Barmen Declaration, II, 2)

Locating the question of reception of BEM as one of those areas in which justification and sanctification are necessary may help us both to take account of the relative importance of the document and, especially, to take account of perspectives which are necessary to understanding the nature of reception.

1. *The document is a major step toward the future catholicity of the church.*

The document is a concise statement of present levels of agreements and continuing challenges to the churches. It is a culmination and a fresh starting point. One does not look to it for novelty or a radical departure in ecumenical relations. Rather, its historical significance is in the way it summarizes and brings to concise formulation a lengthy history of ecumenical discussions at many different levels, including those of bilateral dialogues. There are nuances, surely, to be worked out in each of the topics with which it deals,[2] but it is also an accurate index and reflection of where the participating churches have come in their commitments to the ecumenical movement. Its strength is that it puts in one place and makes explicit the implied commitments of those churches: these are the things about which the participating churches now have to take action one way or another. The document is an accomplishment to be rejoiced in, but it is also one which heightens the *crisis* and makes rather clear that we are

---

[2]There are not just "nuances" to be worked out further, of course. Especially when it comes to the section on ministry, hard clarification and reworking of the language is needed: (a) What is meant by "ordination"? (b) Does the document really intend to mean by "the ordained ministry" what is specified in the next-to-last paragraph of section I ("The Ordained Ministry"), and, if so, what of the ordination to the third of the threefold pattern, and of "elders" in some traditions? (c) What understanding of anthropology and the life of the new humanity is implied in the continued nonordination of women to the special ministry of the Word through proclamation and sacrament?

now dealing with a formulation which demands concrete steps in reception.[3] It
rules out procrastination or avoidance of the admittedly costly and complicated
next steps of official reception for nothing less than concrete, institutional,
structural uniting of the churches. At this point, premature recourse to talk
about a spiritual unity among Christians and churches would be to surface a
docetic ecclesiology.

In making that judgment, I am consciously drawing on the primary theological orientation of which this document in different ways is an outworking. I
mean above all its inescapably trinitarian grounding.[4] The churches' confession
of the triune God has been the single most uniting doctrinal dimension of
Faith and Order's history and of that of the various bilateral conversations. The
decision made early on about the membership of these bodies has been carried
through, so that, even when the doctrine of the Trinity was not the explicit
matter under discussion, it was the organizing assumption. It might be argued,
of course, that that organizing assumption has been a christocentric one, but this
is correct only insofar as the ecumenical movement is in continuity with the
decisions of the first four ecumenical councils that Jesus Christ is the Incarnate
Eternal Word.[5] Moreover, one of the notable features of the document and of
the conversations leading up to it is what the confession of the divinity of the
Holy Spirit means concretely in the empowerment and ordering of the church.
Baptism, eucharist, and ministry are here seen as the outworking in the commu-

---

[3]"Reception" in the present case with BEM is described in the "Recommendation" at
the end of the "Introduction." The churches are to study this document, and, "as concrete
evidence of their ecumenical commitment, the churches are being asked to enable the widest
possible involvement of the whole people of God at all levels of church life in the spiritual
process of receiving this text." This realistic scope of what is meant by "reception" reflects
the North American context, at least, in which (a) education and persuasion are fundamental to how authority is effective and existing at all; (b) different churches assign different
weight to trans-congregational agreement and have different structures even for implementing the request for study; and (c) there is no direct involvement of regional or national
governmental structures in the process. This means that reception in this case is a testing of
the exercise of ecumenical leadership in a highly pluralistic world, where pluralism is not
regretted but accepted as the context of the church's present life and witness.

[4]Cf. not only the baptism in the threefold name but also the doctrine of God presupposed and doxologically expressed in the section on the eucharist.

[5]There is a curious and perhaps self-defeating alliance which may be developing between
those dedicated to liberation movements and those who feel an impatience with or amnesia
about the confession of God's triune Being, and especially about Jesus Christ as fully
anthropos and fully God united in one person. By contrast, G. Gutiérrez' great strength is
the way he holds these two together in the foundational confession and the movement for
liberation. We who are committed to movements of liberation must not let go or minimize
the *homoousios* and the implication of that in the theology worked out in this document.
We need today more than ever to restate and reaffirm Luther's toughness: "I neither have
nor know any other God than the flesh gestated in the womb of the Virgin Mary." The
crucified God is the one who establishes solidarity with all people and empowers men and
women by the resurrection to move from their oppression to new patterns of liberation.
That means that there is a shift of the burden of proof: the question is really how one today
can affirm the doctrine of the Trinity and the *homoousios* and still *not* be committed to
movements of liberation.

nity of believers of the life of the triune God. The process of reception will really be tested by the steadiness with which this fundamental dogmatic decision is carried forward.

Catholicity is indeed partly defined as being in continuity with the decisions of the ecumenical councils. However, the catholicity of the church is as much a future and expanding reality as something which is defined with reference to the past. Allowing the life of the triune God to reshape the community of believers will mean new forms of obedience and new ways of ordering the church in subsequent cultures and among different people: the plenitude of catholicity is ultimately an eschatological reality toward which we are drawn through successive proleptic expressions of it. Subsequent stages of inclusiveness and indigenization of the church's life will involve changes which cannot be discerned or programmed in advance. This means that a major strength of the document is that it is a trajectory of subsequent ecumenism and not just an accurate culmination of Faith and Order and bilateral dialogues to this point.

2. *Understanding the BEM document as promise is an essential ingredient in the process of its reception.*

Churches in different traditions undertake official reception in quite diverse ways and attach differing weights to such reception. I shall say more about that below. Here, I only want to make the point that, no matter at which level and through whatever procedure reception occurs, it is useful to deal with this document as promise and to keep reminding ourselves of the function of promise in the development of the church's catholicity. It is useful because it will help deal with (a) a pattern in the treatment of documents of significant breakthrough, namely, initial enthusiasm followed by discouraged apathy, and (b) what it means for the reception of this document to realize that the church lives by promise.

The first deals with the phenomenon of a certain crisis of credibility as regards the ecumenical movement. There are numerous and complicated reasons for this. Some of these have to do with publicity which gives higher visibility to controversial social and political stands taken by councils of churches than to what occurs in the area of faith and order. It may well be that those stands have to develop a more evenhanded quality, but there is no way the ecumenical movement in its conciliar expression can back away from addressing itself to the injustices about which precisely the church's faith and order must be concerned. I have in mind, however, primarily the dilemma in which persons find themselves who are eager and expectant to see a consequential follow-through from faith and order discussions and an excellent document to concrete, discernible structural changes for greater unity of the churches. We see this, I think, in some of the loss of diminution of enthusiasm which was observable for a while over the Consultation on Church Union, where the transition from a rather carefully worked out document has not yet issued in the kinds of changes among the participating churches for which one might have hoped earlier on.

We have to keep clearly in mind the difference between two models of considering such breakthrough documents. One model is that of an agreement reached which then has only to be applied. This model is one which builds into itself an understandable impatience and then apathy. The other model is that of an agreement which is an index of the trajectory to which we are committed and whose actual reception in practice will occur in ways which are not discernible in advance as one continues to engage in the process. This model corresponds to the way Christians and churches actually live, ideally by trusting the promises of God who draws people forward to the future.

"Promise" can be a vague category because of the way it is often thought of as being in contrast to "fulfillment," in the sense of completion. A different sense of promise emerges when we see it in relation to the initiative and out-working of God's covenanting purposes in the biblical narratives. The relation between covenant and creation is not a minor point. Creation is not merely a given realm in which the histories of the covenants are worked out; rather, Israel's experience of being dealt with by a covenanting God reshapes the very way it appropriates and re-forms prevailing creation sagas to confess the identity between the covenanting God and the Creator. Barth's way of putting this is that creation comes into existence, "is," because God wills to have time and place for another. In this sense, creation itself is an expression of God's covenantal purposes. The promises contained in the covenants have variously to do with what it means to be God's people and the ways God's steadfast love will see to it that there will be a people, even a remnant, as a faithful covenant partner. For a people to interpret its history this way is, by all evident odds, an immense act of daring. What happens could just as well be seen as a series of defeats, thwartings of the promises. The daring interpretation is thàt, through these apparent setbacks, God is actually never letting go of the people and purposes of God but is at work fulfilling those promises in ways which confound and fundamentally alter the criteria by which God's people would judge the promises to be fulfilled. The story—this daringly confessional narrative—is one of a sequence of altered and escalated expectations, a receding horizon, in which at any given moment the promises are only proleptically realized.

It would be a bleak picture, indeed, if all we had to go on was the receding horizon. But, in point of fact, the church confesses that there was "a given moment"—the *ephapax*, "once for all"—when the eschatological fulfillment of the promises broke into history in the coming, death, and resurrection of Jesus the Christ and the uniting to him of a people by the power of the Spirit. The community created, shaped, and enlivened by this eschatological event exists not for itself but precisely as a miracle, an effective sign of God's purposes for all people and all creation. This people moves forward by trust in those promises whose proleptic fulfillment has already been experienced. "Faith" is the word used for this trust informed by Christ's death, resurrection, and the community-creating sending of the Spirit. It is really crucial to get this right, that faith is informed trust as response to the decisive action God has already accomplished in

Christ; otherwise, we mistake faith for credulity, hope for the power of wishful thinking, and love for goodness knows what. The church lives by the promises through faith, but that faith is response to God's decisive accomplishment and is sustained by God's forward-drawing empowerment—in other words, it is response to grace.

This bears directly on the process of reception. We have a long row to hoe in the reception of this document, and the only alternative I know of to a loss of ecumenical nerve is to realize that moving to a greater visible unity of the church is nothing more than the corporate ecclesiastical practice of justification and sanctification by grace alone through faith. I know full well the danger of use of pious language at this point, in such a way that "cheap grace" would displace the "costly grace" of reception. Yet, I am even more aware of how subtle and easy it is to buckle down to more rounds of consultations, bilateral conversations, refining of documents, and information extension—all with "grace aside for the moment." We could easily grant all that technical stuff about grace and justification but "leave it to one side for the moment" and try to advance as if the entire enterprise were not covered by the garment of Christ's righteousness. That is to put it in terms Luther used, but even doctrines of justification which did not use imputed justice as the controlling conviction still held that faith is an active thing from which good works flow.

I have wittingly spoken of both justification *and sanctification* by grace alone through faith in order to underline the point that justification issues forth, is expressed, in sanctification. That means what is at stake in the process of reception is not just the catholicity and unity of the church, but also its holiness. In following the next steps toward which this document points, and in working out its reception, we must be aware that we are moving forward, also, to a greater sanctity of the church. Our respective churches are, at the same time, forgiven and in need of continual forgiveness and correction. The changes we will all confront are not to be seen as exchanging favors or compromising but as witting acts of repentance and welcoming mutual correction in the process of reception to which we are committed. It would be false advertising of this document to say, "Try it; you'll like it!" Ultimately, that will be so, and participants in the process of reception will continue to experience the benefits of these understandings of baptism, eucharist, and ministry. But the process—if we are to take seriously the application of justification and sanctification alone as occurring corporately in the process of reception—will involve "mortification and vivification," death of some cherished structures and new birth, as the church is reshaped to meet the needs of God's own mission to God's own beloved world.[6]

---

[6]This is the import of the ethical implication stated at the end of the third paragraph of the section on baptism in BEM.

3. *Alertness to the interplay between so-called theological and so-called nontheological factors will be important to the process of reception.*

"Theological factors" and "nontheological factors" are not discrete blocks. I have put "so-called" before each to indicate that often the same forces can be viewed theologically and, say, sociologically. There is no theological material which is devoid of sociological shaping and vice versa. By now, this is a truism, but the implications of this for reception are fairly extensive.

One implication is that we should not confidently sort out as "theological" what comes into this document from Christian tradition, and "nontheological" what are contemporary political, economic, and psychological forces. Obviously, the Scriptures and the churches' subsequent doctrinal and organizational development were and will continue in part to be shaped by the cultural contexts of their articulation. The cultural setting of revelation (and I for one still want to insist on the term "revelation") is not to be decried; in fact, it is simply the implication that God's revelation occurs because God chose and chooses to accommodate to our condition.

A second implication is that we should not confidently sort out either set of factors as being inherently unifying or fragmenting in the quest for greater visible unity of the churches. I suppose it is still a fundamental conviction of those engaged in the ecumenical movement that the preponderance of the New Testament materials adds up to a commanding indicative for unity. Apart from this commanding indicative for unity, we and other men and women would find even more reasons, some of them religious, for contentment in our alienation from each other. Even with this, however, there are doctrinal articulations which have furthered, and doctrinal articulations which have hampered, Christian unity. By the same token, so-called nontheological factors work both ways. Perhaps we too often assign nontheological factors a mainly disruptive or disjunctive role at the expense of seeing (to put it confessionally) the way God is also at work drawing Christians together through these so-called nontheological factors.

An example of this is the fact of mixed marriages, which have come with a greater mobility of society. The churches have responded with considerable sluggishness to the de facto situation of serious Christians of different churches joined in marriages—although finally there are some solid indications of a more positive attitude on this matter. What is operative here is the way the practices of faithful Christian men and women present the churches' official teachings with a de facto situation, which then elicits, eventually, a de jure ratification. A good deal of attention has been paid to the way the *lex credendi* is often a response to an existing *lex orandi*. We need, however, to affirm a similar relation between the *lex credendi* and an existing *lex agendi*, the de facto ethical decisions and actions of those witnessing to the power of the gospel for reconciliation and liberation in basic Christian communities. I would not be at all surprised if that were not the import also of the de facto practices of intercommunion at local levels, and not just by members of the same family.[7]

Widespread practice of being the reconciled and reconciling community around the Lord's Table will eventually do as much to elicit doctrinal changes and official reception as the parallel biblical, historical, and dogmatic work which has to go on simultaneously. My only point with regard to mixed marriages and to intercommunion in practice is that Christians are not waiting for official church bodies to make up their minds. De facto precedence of these faithful is an important part of the process of reception in the way it represents a buildup of sociological pressure, which often then elicits and shapes official reception. The same thing is going on when some members in a given congregation feel called to the practice of infant baptism, and others feel called to raise up their children toward baptism as adults. Those two convictions are no longer easily sorted out either in different denominations or in different congregations. People in basic Christian communities are, in point of fact, already drawn to practice the one initiation into the life of Christ and his mission in these two practices. Part of the process of reception will be how seriously and positively we take this de facto situation.

This affects one of the basic questions when it comes to reception: the understanding of authority and actual practice of authority in the contemporary context. The movement is not from above to below—the exercise of authority by handing down a definitive position. (This, I know, is a stereotype of the way even the most hierarchical ordering of the church operated. The actual exercise of authority was far more complicated, and it involved the judgment, at the apex of the pyramid, that what was being defined really represented the devotion of the *congregatio fidelium*.) The situation in which all churches find themselves today is one in which "authority" as a category is almost synonymous with what stands in the way of liberation, or emergence of one's or a people's selfhood, and of a more just redistribution of resources. This does not mean that authority is actually dispensed with, only that it is redefined and exercised in a different way if it is to be effective. The process of reception must take into account this rejection of heteronomous authority, coupled with an immense hunger for an actual practice of authority which makes a freeing and empowering difference in the lives of people.

In making these observations about the interplay of so-called nontheological and theological factors, I am not intending to suggest that we can somehow

---

[7]"De facto intercommunion" is a controversial term which raises the danger of misuse of so-called eucharistic sharing which may bypass both church discipline and the theology contained in carefully examined liturgies. "Eucharistic hospitality" is the term BEM uses for eucharistic fellowship short of full intercommunion. What I mean is the role (essential function) of worshiping together, in a liturgy of eucharist which reflects and expresses the theology of BEM's doctrine of the eucharist, in the process of reception. This is just a variation of the interconnection between the *lex orandi* and the *lex docendi* (and, in this case, the *lex recipiendi*).

bypass the present structures by which churches are governed internally or in the ways they are related to one another. In fact, one would have to look at the current epoch of church history as one in which the Christian movement exhibited a remarkable resilience and a considerable force of leadership in sharing in the rapid social changes of our times. The record on this is spotty, obviously, but at least one of the fruits of the ecumenical movement is the development of new structures for critically evaluating necessary changes and for taking initiative in them, not primarily in response to pressures external to the life of the church, but primarily in response to the dynamic of the gospel. The momentum of reception is finally the inherent power of the gospel, and the only technical questions are those that deal with how we can move forward to make use of breakthrough documents like this so the gospel is served best in our day. Each church has a certain discipline of procedure which is part of the medium through which the message is communicated. Obviously, the point of reception, after all, is not to get a document officially "passed" or "accepted." The point is the transformation of the church in response to the gospel which occurs in the process of reception.

4. *In the foreseeable future, bilateral conversations will continue to play an indispensable role in the process of reception.*

One of the most positive developments has been the close relationship over recent years between work done in bilaterals and the Faith and Order Commission of the World Council of Churches. There was considerable overlap because official observers represented Faith and Order in the major bilaterals at the international level and because a number of personnel were active in both Faith and Order work and the bilaterals. The fruits of discussions in each arena benefited the other, so that substantial input from the bilaterals is also represented in the articulations of this document.[8] The same interchange and parallel cooperation as prevailed in the composition of the document should characterize the process of reception. The history of cooperation on the document suggests that some earlier understandable uneasiness of the division of labor between the W.C.C. and the bilateral work of world confessional families proved to be largely unfounded. We have achieved—in part through the important sessions of the Bilateral Forum, jointly sponsored by the W.C.C. and the theological departments of the world confessional bodies engaged in bilateral discussions—a climate in which the bilaterals can be heartily welcomed and supported as part of the reception process.

---

[8]The material of the numerous bilateral dialogues has been helpfully updated and correlated by the three sessions of the Bilateral Forum and by the continuing bibliographical work of the Centro Pro Unione in Rome. Work done in these bilaterals and the Forum should be made available as resources for the evaluation and further serious study of BEM. Issues opened up and needing careful attention in BEM have a history and a proposed further treatment in the bilaterals and the Forum.

The bilateral conversations have proved beneficial in several ways and will continue to do so. First, the bilaterals are able to deal—in some detail, and with expertise in biblical, historical, systematic, liturgical, and ethical inquiry—with the usually quite technical problems which traditionally have been stumbling blocks between the two partners in dialogue. There can be no shortcutting of the process of this lengthy and technical work. Second, it has been the experience in almost all the bilaterals that certain insights are gained about one's own tradition and that of the other when two churches are in conversation, which do not emerge as readily in other contexts. This phenomenon was quite notable when we sat down to compare and correlate the results of what emerged, for example, when Anglicans were in dialogue with Lutherans. Third, in bilaterals, there has been a momentum of rereading together major texts which have been disputed for centuries and of building on discovered, shared interpretations for the next stages of inquiry. Fourth, the bilaterals provide an important tie of accountability between the persons engaged in the dialogues and the church bodies officially authorizing them. As the conversations between two churches proceed, there occurs a growth of understanding, not just between representatives of two different traditions but also within the enabling churches themselves. Fifth, and perhaps most importantly, the bilaterals enable participants to confront and deal with controversial and emotionally laden issues in a context of partnership, where each side needs the other perspective in tough dialogue. This will be true in pursuing the implications of this document for baptism and eucharist—but especially in the arduous work we have before us for years, on the doctrine and ordering of ministry.

Here I have in mind especially the tough decisions and unparalleled opportunity facing the churches on the matter of ordaining women to the special ministry of the Word through proclamation and sacraments. Much ground still has to be covered on topics which have been on the agenda of faith and order discussion for years, but those topics can no longer be dealt with to the exclusion of dealing with the ordination of women to the special ministry. In some of the bilaterals, this is not yet even a matter for serious discussion, even though the discussion partners may be those on one side for whom the ordination of women is almost inconceivable, and those on the other side for whom the ordination of women is a necessary obedience to the gospel in our time.[9] Mutual

---

[9]There are fundamental dogmatic imperatives for the ordination of human beings, men and women, to the special ministry. Those who favor such ordination often treat it on prudential grounds or on the ground that it is necessary to carry through into the life of the church the gains of the civil-rights movement. The somewhat minimal argument is also advanced that women have gifts to do the task of ministry—which has already been defined in predominantly male categories. However, the fundamental dogmatic imperative is from the life of the triune God who creates humanity as co-humanity: the refusal of ministry in all levels to this co-humanity is a broken witness to the accomplished work and empowering presence of the Eternal Word who assumed humanity's condition. Here the Tradition which confesses the doctrines of the Trinity and Incarnation is not incidental or disposable, but it is precisely the material for the hermeneutical process. The language of BEM at this point

recognition of ministry in this situation will necessitate the kinds of discussions which can best be pursued in bilateral dialogues in which there is a high degree of accountability to the respective churches and the necessary longevity for detailed inquiry.

It is encouraging to see a number of bilateral dialogues entering their second and third round at the international, national, and regional levels. In some cases, these have become so much a part of the theological work at these levels that the dialogue partnership has become almost a permanent part of each church's own growth. We are, however, at a stage where two things must occur in the process of reception. First, the present level of bilateral discussions must be maintained, and other conversations must be initiated. Churches need these periodically to keep pace with how each is changing. We must also seek to bring into these conversations churches which have not been involved much before. It is not necessary that all these occur at the national level. In fact, we need to take seriously the work which often is done for the church at large by significantly pioneering work in regional bilateral and multilateral conversations. Second, we need improved ways of sharing the results of these conversations as they occur. It would be useful to have regular ways of assuring that the various bilateral conversations on international, national, and regional levels were kept abreast of each other. Many exceptionally fine lines of progress are being opened up at one level that are unknown at other levels.

I should think it would be useful to have something analogous to the Bilateral Forum to deal with bilateral conversations on the North American scene as the Bilateral forum did internationally. That was not developed into a permanent office, nor does this suggestion envisage a permanent office. The point would be, rather, to have an occasion to assemble a few representative participants in bilaterals in North America for the purpose of updating and evaluating where the bilaterals have come thus far and their usefulness on specific issues in the progress of reception.

---

is just too weak, precisely because it does not follow through on the implications of the trinitarian groundwork: "An increasing number of churches have decided that there are no biblical or theological reasons against ordaining women, and many of them have subsequently proceeded to do so. Yet many churches hold that the tradition of the Church in this regard must not be changed" (BEM, Ministry, 2; II). What "tradition" is referred to here is a special question: is not "the traditions" meant, rather than "Tradition"? The task of hermeneutics of the apostolic faith in its ecumenical-conciliar expression requires reformulation, but, were we to lose the trinitarian character of whatever metaphors we use, the dogmatic foundation of genuine liberation and empowerment of all humans for ministry would be undercut.

BAPTISM, EUCHARIST, AND MINISTRY:
THE RECEPTION OF THE TEXT
AND THIRD WORLD CONCERNS

J. Russell Chandran

I join with the large number of people in churches throughout the world in rejoicing in the *Baptism, Eucharist, and Ministry* (hereafter, BEM) document, which represents an important breakthrough in the modern ecumenical quest for the visible unity of the church. It has been mentioned repeatedly that the document is the result of more than a half century of ecumenical dialogue. It will, however, be appropriate to remember that the concern for manifesting the oneness of the church was first expressed with a sense of urgency in the mission frontier of a Third World situation. It was William Carey, the Baptist missionary in India, facing the scandal for his evangelistic mission of a divided church, who proposed an ecumenical conference of missionary organizations to be held at the Cape of Good Hope in 1810. I regard the BEM document as a significant contribution to the fulfillment of the vision of the relation between the oneness of the church and the mission to which Christ has called the church.

The discussions and study which resulted in the adoption of the BEM document may be traced back to the very first meeting of the Faith and Order conference held at Lausanne in 1927. However, the effort to produce a document for the common affirmation by all churches on baptism, eucharist, and ministry belongs to the later period following the Lund conference of 1952, when there was a shift in Faith and Order methodology from that of comparative ecclesiology to that of discovering what the churches were called to hold in common. I was a member of the Faith and Order Commission for more than two decades after 1952, and I recall how difficult the process was of arriving at what could be commonly affirmed. The history of the Faith and Order discussions

J. Russell Chandran (Church of South India) has been Principal and Professor of Theology and Ethics at United Theological College in Bangalore, India, since 1954, prior to which he was a lecturer at United Theological College from 1950. Ordained in 1946, he served as pastor of a rural congregation in South Travancore, 1945-47. He has been a visiting professor at Union Theological Seminary, New York; Presbyterian Theological Seminary, Louisville; Episcopal Theological School, Cambridge, MA; the Lutheran School of Theology and McCormick Theological Seminary, Chicago; and for 1983-84 at Trinity Lutheran Seminary, Columbus, OH. He holds an M.A. in Math from Madras University, a B.D. from United Theological College, a B.Litt. from Mansfield College, Oxford, and an S.T.M. from Union Theological Seminary (1950), with additional study at the Divinity School of the University of Chicago (1957-58). He has been a member of the Faith and Order Commission of the W.C.C. (1952-63), a member of the W.C.C. Central Committee and its Executive Committee, and Vice Chairman of the W.C.C. He has attended all W.C.C. Assemblies and numerous other ecumenical gatherings, guest-lectured at seminaries and universities throughout Europe and the U.S.A., and served on many Indian and Asian church and peace organizations. His articles have appeared in several scholarly journals.

from Lausanne onward also clearly indicates that baptism, eucharist, and ministry are the three main areas on which churches have had the most difficult differences of beliefs and practices. In quite a number of the church-union negotiations also—such as those which led to the formation of the Church of North India, those between the Church of South India and both Lutherans and Baptists, and other conversations—agreements on baptism, eucharist, and ministry have been crucial.

My reflection on the document from a Third World perspective is certainly subject to some limitations. Even though through my participation in the ecumenical movement and my association with the Ecumenical Association of Third World Theologians I am aware of the broader concerns of churches in the Third World, I cannot really claim to represent all Third World concerns. I have to limit myself to perspectives from my knowledge of churches in Asia and particularly in India.

The Asian Context

The context of the church's life and mission in the Third World, particularly in Asia, is marked by certain glaring facts. The first is the most visible fact of mass poverty alongside affluence and the concentration of wealth in the hands of a few. The conditions of misery to which vast masses of people in Asia, in both urban and rural areas, are subjected are a disgrace to human dignity. The second important fact is that most of the Asian people live by religions other than Christianity. In the whole of Asia, with almost half of the world's population, only about four percent are Christian. In most of Asia the percentage of Christians is much smaller; in some countries it is less than one percent, and there are regions with almost no Christians at all. The church's mission is also challenged by the rival claims of other religions such as Islam, Buddhism, and Hinduism to have more relevant gospels to meet the needs of personal salvation and the global struggle for peace. Third, there are different forms of struggle against the unjust conditions and oppressive structures in different countries. The India Social Institute in Bangalore and the Christian Institute for the Study of Religion and Society have made some case studies of a number of such struggles in India. The socio-political discontent of people has also in several situations been expressed in violent conflicts such as in the Philippines, Sri Lanka, Pakistan, and Assam and Punjab in India. The situation in Lebanon, in Afghanistan, in Iran, and the Iran-Iraq war are also to be understood in terms of the people's struggle for peace with justice.

As the church lives and witnesses in the context of such a complexity of factors, its image is often very ambiguous. While many continue to recognize the contribution of the service institutions of the church, the question of whether the church or the Christian community in Asia is seen as having a significant role does not have a clear answer. The divided state of the church and the dependence on the West of quite a number of churches for financial support as well as denominational loyalty have added to the weakening of the church's image. In most situations the call to people for conversion to the Christian faith, renouncing their original religion, is resented as having anti-national and harmful socio-political consequences. Even though in several situations the church's mission had challenged unjust practices, on the whole the image of the church is one of supporting the status quo rather than of transforming the socio-political structures.

In this context, however, the movements for unity represented by both the ecumenical organizations, such as the Christian Conference of Asia, and the church union movements have given a new direction to the churches for the renewal of their image. The movement for unity has been associated with a new sensitivity to relating the mission of the church to the struggles of the people for a more meaningful human existence, taking into consideration the religious, spiritual, cultural, and socio-political dimensions of the struggle. This concern was expressed by the recently formed Joint Council of the Church of North India, the Church of South India, and the Mar Thoma Church by stating one of the Council's objectives as: "to help the churches to fulfil the mission of evangelization of the people of India and of witnessing to the righteousness of God revealed in the Gospel of Jesus Christ by striving for a just society."

The Receiving of the BEM Document

How do the churches involved in such a context receive the BEM document? Certainly, the churches in Asia and in other Third World countries receive the document with a sense of joyous thanksgiving for God's guidance in enabling the Faith and Order Commission to arrive at this document. At the same time the churches will also be realistic in their acceptance of the status and role of the document. First, it has to be borne in mind that the document is not a systematic and comprehensive formulation of the doctrines of baptism, eucharist, and ministry, nor was it intended to deal with all the theological questions related to these subjects. Its objective was only to deal with the differences and misunderstandings among the churches in faith and practice relating to baptism, eucharist, and ministry which have developed over the centuries and have kept the churches divided. Second, while this document marks an important and history-making achievement in the quest for the visible unity of the church, it does not yet represent the final goal. This is clearly acknowledged in the Preface of the document. The director and moderator of the Commission, William H. Lazareth and Nikos Nissiotis, respectively, have stated, "Certainly we have not yet fully reached consensus (*consentire*), understood here as that experience of life and articulation of faith necessary to realize and maintain the Church's visible unity. . . . Full consensus can only be proclaimed after the churches reach the point of living and acting together in unity."[1] Third, it has also been pointed out clearly that the official responses to the document from the churches will be considered at a future World Conference on Faith and Order. This envisages another stage of Faith and Order work before the final consensus linked with the manifestation of the visible unity of the church.

Such a realistic assessment of the document, however, does not minimize the importance of the document for an experience of renewal in the churches and growth of mutual understanding among the churches to be expected through the process of reception of the document. The Preface, therefore, rightly describes the receiving of the text as a "spiritual process" and calls upon the churches "to enable the widest possible involvement of the whole people of God." This would mean that the churches receive the document not only with realism but also with hope, hope of renewal and of moving forward for the fulfillment of the vision of unity which Christ has given to the church. In the hope of renewal, churches need to receive the document with plans for its study by different groups within each church and also for joint study by groups representing several churches in a locality or region. In this regard the churches will do well to take seriously the recommendations from the consultation on United and Uniting Churches held at Colombo in 1981, under the auspices of the Faith and Order Commission of the World Council of Churches, and also from the meetings of representatives from the Colombo Consultation both with the Vatican Secretariat for Promoting Christian Unity at Rome, and with members of Orthodox churches at Chambesy, in February, 1983.

The members of the Colombo Consultation said:

> We commit ourselves to strengthen the linkage provided through the W.C.C. by listening more carefully to the voices we hear in that forum, by responding more seriously to the products of the multilateral search for consensus (such as the forthcoming statement on Baptism, Eucharist and the Ministry), and by articulating more clearly for others the distinctive experiences and perspectives of United churches.[2]

At the Colombo Consultation, Bishop Lakshman Wickramasinghe reminded the participants that the united and uniting churches were, on the whole, of Protestant orientation and that for wholeness of the unity of the church they needed to be enriched by the insights and experiences of the Roman Catholic, Orthodox, and Pentecostal churches.[3]

---

[1]*Baptism, Eucharist, and Ministry*, Faith and Order Paper 111 (Geneva: World Council of Churches, 1982), Preface, p. ix.

[2]*Growing towards Consensus and Commitment*, Faith and Order Paper 110 (Geneva: World Council of Churches, 1981), p. 22.

[3]Ibid., pp. 70-73.

The meeting at Rome made specific reference to the BEM document:

The doctrinal convergence on Baptism, Eucharist and the Ministry, achieved through Faith and Order, is an important reference point for union negotiations, united churches and churches engaged in bilateral conversations. All will be challenged to reflect on their understanding of the sacraments and ministry by this multilateral document.[4]

The recommendations from this meeting are addressed to both the Roman Catholic Church and the united and uniting churches. They include the following: (a) The Secretariat for Promoting Christian Unity should find appropriate ways of encouraging local churches to enter into dialogue and cooperation with united churches and union committees in order that these local expressions of unity may not be isolated from universal concerns nor universal concerns be pursued without reference to local needs. It is in this setting that the churches should make a further study of the concept of "unity by stages." (b) The united churches and church union committees should explore increased contact with traditions not involved in direct union negotiations, such as the Roman Catholic Church. The Faith and Order Commission was asked to facilitate this exploration.[5] These recommendations certainly suggest that the BEM document can be the basis for fresh interchurch contacts for mutual understanding, correction, enrichment, and growth toward making visible the fullness of the unity of the church.

Suggestions for the Process of Study

The study process will first look at what the document enables the churches to affirm together on baptism, eucharist, and ministry. This will help the churches to see how the document has brought to light the great measure of unity which already exists among the churches. Second, the study will consider the call for mutual understanding among the churches for the diversities of practice and belief relating to the sacraments and the ministry. Third, there is need to work out the theological and practical implications of what the document says. As admitted in the Preface, the language of the document is "largely classical in reconciling historical controversies." Therefore, it needs to be translated and reformulated to make the affirmations more challengingly relevant for contemporary situations, locally as well as globally. Fourth, the study should also consider questions not adequately dealt with in the document.

---

[4]Michael Kinnamon, ed., *Unity in Each Place . . . in All Places*, Faith and Order Paper 118 (Geneva: W.C.C., 1983), p. 46.
[5]Ibid., p. 49.

The Oneness of the Faith Affirmations

The document begins with the affirmation that baptism is rooted in the ministry of Jesus, then expounds the meaning of the sacrament. The emphasis of the document is that the basic reality in the sacrament is what God has done for us in the life, death, and resurrection of Jesus Christ and in the gift of the Holy Spirit. Baptism is participation in the life, death, and resurrection of Christ, breaking the power of sin, and the entrance into a new life. Baptism calls for confession of sin and conversion, and the baptized are pardoned, cleansed, and sanctified by Christ. The Holy Spirit guides them to a new ethical orientation. Describing baptism as the sign of the reign of God, it is affirmed that the sacrament has the dynamic which embraces the whole of life, extends to all nations, and anticipates the day when all will confess that Jesus Christ is Lord. It is pointed out that churches regard baptism both as a gift from God and as demanding the response of faith and commitment. It is further affirmed that baptism is related not only to the momentary experience but to lifelong growth into the likeness of Christ. The baptized live in hope of the new creation and of the time when God will be all in all. Another important affirmation is that baptism is an unrepeatable act.

Of the eucharist, also, there is a brief historical account which points out that the eucharist is a "gift from the Lord"[6] and that the church continues to celebrate it as the central act of worship. The meaning of the eucharist is expounded as expressing the trinitarian faith of the church. It is the great thanksgiving to God, the *anamnesis* or memorial of Christ, and invokes the Holy Spirit. The eucharist is the sacrament of the unique sacrifice of Christ and the memorial of all that God has done for the salvation of the world. The words and acts of Christ at the institution of the eucharist are at the heart of the celebration. The eucharistic meal is the sacrament of the body and blood of Christ and, therefore, the sacrament of the real presence of Christ. All churches agree that, while the real presence of Christ in the eucharist does not depend on the faith of the individual, faith is required for the discernment of the body and blood of Christ. In the section on the eucharist as the "Communion of the Faithful," it is affirmed that it is in the eucharist that the community of God's people is fully manifested and that, insofar as the whole church is involved in each local eucharistic celebration, each local church has to order its own life in ways which take seriously the interests and concerns of other churches.

Affirming that the eucharist embraces all aspects of life, the document draws attention to all kinds of injustices which are radically challenged when we share in the body and blood of Christ. The obstinacy of unjustifiable confessional oppositions within the body of Christ are also identified as inconsistent with the celebration of the eucharist. Describing the eucharist as the meal of the reign of God, Christians are also reminded of the eschatological vision of the final

---

[6]BEM, Eucharist, Par. 1.

renewal of creation. The eucharist is the feast at which the church has a foretaste of the reign and looks forward to its coming. Eucharistic participation in Christ is also a call to be in solidarity with the outcast and to become signs of the love of Christ. The eucharist is further described as a new reality transforming Christians into the image of Christ, making them his effective witnesses.

Participation in God's mission is an integral dimension of eucharistic celebration, and this is also a challenge to the eucharistic assembly to be concerned to gather into the one body those who are at present beyond its visible limits, because Christ invited to his feast all for whom he died. In this regard it is frankly acknowledged that, insofar as Christians cannot unite in full fellowship around the same table to eat the same loaf and drink from the same cup, their missionary witness is weakened at both the individual and the corporate levels. The importance of the liturgical movement for the renewal of the eucharistic celebration in the churches is recognized, and it is recommended both that churches should celebrate the eucharist frequently and that every Christian should be encouraged to receive communion frequently.

In interchurch relations the most difficult problems have been associated with the ordained ministry, so it is remarkable that the BEM document includes a section indicating a large measure of agreement and convergence. At the outset, however, it is pointed out that, though the churches are agreed in their general understanding of the calling of the people of God, they differ in their understanding of how the life of the church is to be ordered. It is admitted that the main problems are in relation to the place and forms of the ordained ministry, but it is agreed that in the efforts to overcome those differences the churches need to work from the perspective of the calling of the whole people of God. It is the whole people of God who are called to be involved in the continuing ministry and mission of Jesus Christ. It is in the context of the calling of the whole people of God that the specific role of ordained ministry is to be seen.

The document is concerned with the question of finding a common answer to the problems about the ordained ministry. There is agreement about the need for an ordained ministry. It is affirmed that ordained ministers can fulfill their calling only in and for the community. They have to be recognized by the community. The authority of the ordained minister is rooted in Jesus Christ, who has received it from the Father, and who confers it by the Holy Spirit through the act of ordination. The concept of priesthood associated with the ordained ministry is also related to the understanding of Jesus Christ as the unique priest of the new covenant and the understanding of the consequent priesthood of the whole church. The ordained ministers, however, may appropriately be called priests because they fulfill a particular priestly service by strengthening and building up the royal and prophetic priesthood of the faithful through word and sacraments, through their prayers of intercession, and through their pastoral guidance of the community.

In spite of differences of understanding of the traditional threefold ministry of bishops, presbyters, and deacons, a great measure of agreement is recorded. At the same time it is affirmed that the threefold pattern evidently stands in need of reform. As guiding principles for the exercise of the ordained ministry the document suggests that three dimensions should be preserved, namely, the personal, the collegial, and the communal, and that the ordained ministry needs to be constitutionally or canonically ordered and exercised in the church in such a way that each of these dimensions can find adequate expression. It is also agreed that the exercise of the ordained ministry should be in a manner which safeguards the active participation of all members in the decision-making of the community. Recognizing the diversity of gifts the Holy Spirit gives for the enrichment of the life of the church, the ordained ministry needs to be so exercised that it does not become a hindrance to the variety of these charisms.

With regard to the controversial question of succession in the apostolic tradition, the document has recorded an important agreement. The church lives in continuity with the Apostles and their proclamation. It is the Holy Spirit who keeps the church in the apostolic tradition until the fulfillment of history in the reign of God. The primary manifestation of apostolic succession is to be found in the apostolic tradition of the church as a whole. The succession is an expression of the permanence and, therefore, of the continuity of Christ's own mission in which the church participates. This is recognized as a critical principle for reviewing and reforming the structure of the ordained ministry.

Call for Mutual Understanding

The document acknowledges that in the course of history a diversity of forms have developed in the understanding and practice of the sacraments and the ministry, and these have contributed to the divisions among the churches. Mutual understanding among the churches can lead to mutual acceptance of diverse beliefs and practices so that the divisions may be overcome.

In relation to baptism two major issues have been identified. The first is the division between churches practicing infant baptism and those baptizing only believers who are able to make a personal confession of faith. It is noted that the churches which baptize children provide for the personal response of faith at a later moment in life; therefore, for all the churches, the baptized person has to grow in the understanding of faith. It is also noted that churches baptize believers coming from other religions or from unbelief as converts to the Christian faith.

There is a convergence of understanding of the baptismal practices and beliefs; as a result, churches are increasingly recognizing one another's baptism as the one baptism into Christ. The document, therefore, recommends that wherever possible mutual recognition should be expressed explicitly by the churches. In this connection it is good to recall that in the Church of North India, which came into being in 1970, churches practicing infant baptism and those practicing believers' baptism went beyond the stage of mutual recognition of each other's baptism and became united in one church. In this church both believers' baptism and infant baptism are practiced. Infant baptism is followed later by confirmation when the person makes an affirmation of faith. In the case of believers' baptism there is a service of dedication of infants, witnessing to the faith that children born in Christian homes belong to Christ and are to be brought up in the knowledge of Christ. In no case is the baptism to be repeated. In the conversations between the Church of South India and the Baptist churches in South India there has been general agreement that the churches could unite on the same basis as the Church of North India. It is for other reasons that the union conversations have been stalled.

The second issue is related to the association of chrismation and confirmation with baptism. The Eastern churches developed the practice of anointing with chrism as symbolic of the gift of the Holy Spirit. The churches of the Western tradition developed the rite of confirmation with the laying on of hands as a sign of the gift of the Holy Spirit. It is pointed out that differences of traditions need not perpetuate disunity. Almost all churches agree that baptism is in water and the Holy Spirit. With such mutual understanding, common acceptance of baptism, irrespective of the diversities of practices, should be possible.

With regard to the eucharist it is pointed out that many differences of theology, liturgy, and practice determine the frequency with which the Holy Communion is celebrated. In awareness of such differences, the need for frequent celebration is affirmed. The situation calls for mutual learning from the different theological and liturgical points of view for a more meaningful celebration of the Risen Lord through the eucharist. Another problem concerns the way in which the elements are treated. Some churches stress that Christ's presence in the consecrated elements continues after the celebration, and, therefore, the elements must be treated accordingly. Other churches emphasize the presence of Christ in the act of celebration itself and in the consumption of the elements in the act of communion. The document calls for mutual understanding and respect for the different practices. These differences should not stand in the way of churches' attaining a greater measure of eucharistic communion and moving toward the day when all Christ's people will be visibly united around the Lord's Table.

The most difficult problem in the area of ministry is the mutual recognition of the ordained ministries of churches possessing the historic episcopate and those which do not. In spite of these difficulties the document has indicated directions for the churches to move in order to achieve mutual recognition. It is suggested that churches in ecumenical conversations can recognize their respective ordained ministers if they are mutually assured of their intention to transmit the ministry of Word and Sacrament in continuity with apostolic times. The practical steps to be taken to achieve mutual recognition by churches which have preserved the episcopal succession and those which have not are taken from the experiences of churches which have united or been involved in union conversations. The goal is to recover the sign of episcopal succession without making any negative judgment on the apostolic content of the ordained ministry existing in churches without the episcopal succession. This was how the Church of South India became a church with the historic episcopate and at the same time incorporated into its ministry those who had been ordained in the nonepiscopal churches coming into the union. It was assumed that, because the churches became united in one episcopally ordered church in obedience to God, the ministries also had been united; therefore, no separate unification rite for the ministry was adopted. In the Church of North India, however, which had a similar problem, the ministries were united through a special unification rite with mutual laying on of hands.

Another difficult problem for mutual recognition of ministries is related to the ordination of women. The document points out that all churches believe that in Christ all barriers are broken down, including the gender barrier, yet different churches draw different conclusions as to the admission of women to the ordained ministry. However, it also records the agreement that the obstacles raised by this issue must not be regarded as substantive hindrance for further efforts toward mutual recognition. Both the Church of North India and the Church of South India have accepted the ordination of women. The Mar Thoma Church does not accept women for ordination, but the three churches are united in a Joint Council, affirming that they belong together in one church because of their common faith and mutual recognition of one another's sacraments and ministry. Even though the Mar Thoma Church does not ordain women, and there is no move yet in that church to consider the question, the C.N.I. and C.S.I. action has not created any problem for the Joint Council. This is partly because of the priority of making visible the organic oneness which the three churches believe is the gift of God in Christ. The fact that the Mar Thoma Church is in communion with the Anglican Church, several provinces of which ordain women, may also be a factor in its attitude toward the ordination of women.

Exploration of the Implications

I would like to draw attention to a few statements in the BEM document whose meaning and implications need to be explored and reinterpreted.

In the section on baptism there is an emphasis on the ethical implications of the sacrament. In Par. 4, part of the baptismal experience is a new ethical orientation under the guidance of the Holy Spirit. Again, in Par. 10, baptism understood as baptism into Christ's death is affirmed as having ethical implications which call not only for personal sanctification but also for the striving for the realization of the will of God in all realms of life. Ethical orientation associated with religious initiation is not unique to Christianity. Hinduism, Islam, Buddhism, and other religions have a strong emphasis on the ethical implications of the religious life. There are also those who would regard ethics, particularly the ethic of love, as the key to the truth in all religions and, therefore, advocate the harmony of religions and oppose conversion from one religion to another. In this context what we mean by the ethical orientation which baptism gives needs to be spelled out. What difference does baptism affirmed as incorporation into the Body of Christ make for the quality of life which a person lives in different situations today? For proper understanding of the ethical orientation brought about by baptism, one needs to look at two other important affirmations in the document, namely, that Jesus was baptized in solidarity with sinners (Par. 3) and that baptism is baptism into Christ's death (Par. 10, 12).

If our baptism is incorporation into Christ, the meaning of Jesus' baptism is important for the understanding of our baptism. In the evangelist's testimony, Jesus received John's baptism, given to sinners for the remission of sins, even though *he* did not need remission of sin. He received the baptism for the fulfillment of God's righteousness (Mt. 3:15). In doing so he stood in solidarity with sinful humanity seeking forgiveness, thus demonstrating the power of God's righteousness, bringing about an inclusive corporateness of the oneness of new humanity. In Christ's practice of solidarity with sinners, all forms of exclusiveness are overcome. Thus baptism has become a sacrament of inclusive unity, rejecting all forms of divisiveness and exclusiveness. Therefore, a baptized person is committed to belong in Christ to the corporateness of the new humanity and deliberately seeks to overcome the human solidarities which are divisive of the human community, such as caste, class, race, language, nationality, and religious denomination. This dimension of inclusiveness and corporateness is often not understood by those receiving baptism or by those bringing children for baptism.

In connection with a consultation on baptism by the Faith and Order unit of the National Council of Churches in India, I participated in a study on the meaning and practice of baptism along with a few of my colleagues on the Faculty of the United Theological College, Bangalore. For this we did a limited survey of the practice in several of the churches in India. We found that the primary emphasis in almost all the documents examined was on the function of baptism as a means of saving grace for the individual baptized. The hymns and lyrics used at baptismal services are those which pray for individualistic grace and freedom from sin. References to baptism as a commitment to a life of discipleship and service within the corporate human community are rather minimal and almost negligible. This may not be true of the situation in other countries. However, it is important that in interpreting baptism the corporateness of our solidarity in Christ be stressed.

The understanding of baptism in terms of Christ's death brings out another equally important dimension. In Lk. 12:50, Jesus describes his death as a baptism he had to undergo. The manner in which Jesus worked out the implications of the solidarity of his baptism led him to the cross. When the BEM document states that the baptized are called upon to reflect the glory of the Lord, we need to remember that according to the fourth evangelist his glory was seen in his suffering and death. It was through his utter obedience to the will of the Father that he demonstrated the power of his love in the powerlessness of dying on the cross, in his identification with the victims of sinful abuse of power. The relation between baptism and Christ's death also challenges us to ask how in the different situations today the baptized are to make this real. How this is to be done has to be discerned by the churches in each age and in different situations.

For the assembly of the Christian Conference of Asia, held in Bangalore in May, 1982, the main theme was "Living in Christ with the People." In expounding this theme, one of the concerns was to see how participation in Christ challenged the churches to express their solidarity with the oppressed and suffering peoples of Asia. The suffering and death of Christ enable us to understand the sufferings of the oppressed and of those involved in the struggle for justice and liberation from oppression. It is also through the knowledge and experience of suffering in the cause of righteousness in contemporary situations that we are able to gain a deeper understanding of the meaning of the cross of Jesus Christ. Without such solidarity in Christ with the people, the affirmation of our participation in the resurrection of Christ may become naive and triumphalistic.

For mutual recognition of baptism the document rightly recommends that churches practicing infant baptism must guard themselves against the practice of apparently indiscriminate baptism (Par. 16). In most situations the baptism of children has become part of the culture, and the churches do not always require any conditions other than the parents' desire that the children should be baptized. The survey in India showed that in the churches baptizing infants there is hardly any arrangement for the preparation of either the parents or the sponsors/godparents. Neither did we find in churches practicing adult or believers' baptism any organized plan or materials to prepare the candidates for baptism. In quite a number of churches, preparation consists only in the teaching of the Ten Commandments, the Lord's Prayer, and the Apostles' Creed. In some of the churches in North East India, however, elders interview the candidates for baptism, and a personal public confession of their faith is required. In order to make mutual recognition meaningful and baptismal unity of the churches a real unity in Christ, it is important that churches make adequate provision for preparing the candidates or the parents/sponsors bringing children for baptism, as well as for continued nurture for growth in faith and in the Christian style of life.

Another recommendation in the document which has practical implications is that baptism should always be celebrated in the setting of the Christian community (Par. 12) and that it should usually be administered during public worship (Par. 23). This means that, normally, private baptism is to be discouraged. The Indian survey indicated that in many churches the practice of private baptism continues for those who could afford the required fees, either in homes or in places of worship without a public gathering of the congregation. This practice certainly distorts the meaning of baptism and encourages the understanding of the sacrament as a private, individualistic affair. Deliberate steps have to be taken by the churches to prevent this distortion and to make baptism an event of the whole congregation in which a person, infant or adult, is received as a member, and to make it an occasion for the whole congregation to be renewed with fresh commitment to baptismal solidarity in and with Christ.

The commentary on Par. 21 has raised the question of the appropriateness of the practice in some parts of the world of requiring the newly baptized to assume names which are not rooted in their cultural tradition. It is noted that this has led to confusion between baptism and customs surrounding name-giving. Even though the practice of name-changing has a very long history in several religions, it is important to recognize that the practice of the assumption of new names by the baptized in the Christian churches to demonstrate their new identity has led to serious problems. It strengthened the impression that Christians were alienated from the indigenous culture and belonged to another culture. In India this has practical consequences today for Christians from the lower "scheduled" castes. They have found the foreign names an obvious disadvantage when seeking benefits from the government's policy of preferential discrimination to help members of the "scheduled" castes. The situation has encouraged many to renounce their baptism and to adopt their earlier names or new Hindu names. There are some, however, who change their Christian names but continue in the fellowship of the church. Even apart from this particular problem, the practice of assuming names for giving a separate Christian identity distinct from the cultural identity of those among whom the church has to live and witness needs to be critically reviewed.

What is the distinctive mark of the people incorporated into Christ? Is cultural separation a necessary consequence of baptism? In this connection also churches need to consider the implications of the new ethical orientation and the inclusiveness of solidarity with the people which Christ brings to the baptized. The separation which baptism in Christ really brings is not from names and external forms, but from the spirit of separation and exclusiveness and from conformity with a way of life which supports unjust structures and which is indifferent to the needs of others.

The unrepeatable character of baptism (Par. 13) needs further explanation. The problem in India and possibly in many other parts of the world is not only with regard to mutual recognition by churches. Individuals seek rebaptism because of doubts about the validity or efficacy of the earlier baptism. This is largely due to the emphasis of sectarian groups and revival preachers on the emotional personal experience of receiving the Holy Spirit and of salvation. The Indian survey showed that people seek rebaptism for the following reasons: the merit and popularity of the one who baptizes, doubts about the form and mode of the previous baptism administered in the church, the level of conviction and spiritual state of the baptized, and the expectation of personal experience of spiritual assurances and gifts.

It was also seen that many cases of rebaptism are related to the impression given in many churches that water baptism does not bring the gift of the Holy Spirit and that the receiving of the Holy Spirit is only at the time of confirmation with the laying on of hands. This is certainly a distortion and has to be overcome by more adequate teaching and restoration of the unity of the sacrament of Christian initiation. The practice of the Orthodox churches has much to teach us in this matter. The unrepeatability of baptism needs to be interpreted by the affirmation that in baptism God's faithfulness in what has been done for us in Christ is the decisive act, and not our response of faith. Seeking rebaptism implies questioning God's faithfulness and so is contrary to the right understanding of the sacrament. Churches should provide other means whereby members may have occasions to renew their response of faith and regain their assurance of belonging to Christ.

Another point for further elucidation is the kind of reform needed in the pattern of the threefold ministry of bishop, presbyter, and deacon. I would like to draw attention to the place of the diaconate (Ministry, Par. 24 and 31). The document recognizes the ambiguity of the position of deacons in many churches. However, no clear guidance is given for the kind of reform toward which churches may move for a more meaningful expression of the threefold ministry. The affirmation that deacons represent to the church its calling as servant in the world and that, by struggling in Christ's name with the myriad needs of societies and persons, deacons exemplify the interdependence of worship and service in the church's life (Par. 31) may be taken as a key for the restoration of the diaconate to its rightful place within the threefold ministry.

During the last few decades many churches have expressed concern about the unsatisfactory manner in which the diaconate is treated within the ministry. The Church of South India, which took the traditional form of the threefold ministry, soon found that, unless the diaconate was given a distinctive role, its place in a threefold ministry would have no meaning. The question was taken up for study by the Theological Commission of the Church of South India. It was noted that the Roman Catholic Church also had started raising questions about the traditional form of the diaconate. Vatican II proposed reorganizing the diaconate as a permanent or lifetime ministry. This certainly goes a long way toward giving the diaconate a more meaningful place, but not far enough. Even in the revised structure the diaconate is a somewhat subordinate and inferior office.

At the request from the Church of South India as well as other churches, the Faith and Order Commission of the W.C.C. took up the subject of the diaconate for ecumenical study.[7] The study, led by Lukas Vischer, made it clear that the form of the diaconate as it evolved in the Western tradition was unsatisfactory and was in need of reinterpretation. A consultation on the diaconate, organized jointly by the Faith and Order Commission and the Laity Department of the W.C.C. in 1965, made the following affirmations: (1) The diaconate is a ministry with a special character of its own. It is not proper to maintain it as an auxiliary function. (2) The diaconate should not become an autonomous

---

[7]The study report appeared in *Encounter*, vol. 25, no. 1 (1964).

ministry isolated from the other ministries. The ministries in the church are all interrelated and form a unity witnessing to the one ministry of Christ. (3) Close connection between worship of God and service of one's neighbor is not clearly expressed in the way any one church is ordered. In many churches of the Reformation a diaconate has been developed which has as its function the fulfillment of important welfare tasks. This raises the question of the relation of the diaconate to liturgical life.

The trend in the Church of South India, particularly under the guidance of its Theological Commission, has been to understand the diaconate as expressing Christ's compassionate ministry. Christ's ministry cannot be understood merely as welfare or charity or first aid; rather, his ministry witnessed to the righteousness of God. Accordingly, it is suggested that the diaconate should represent the church's social concern, not simply what is normally included in the term "social services," but a concern which will involve the church in the struggles of the people for justice. Nothing very significant has emerged yet, but the discussion continues. The BEM document does affirm the church's calling to be involved in the struggle for justice (Eucharist, Par. 20; Ministry, Par. 4). If churches work out the implications of these affirmations for the reordering of the ministry, a meaningful renewal of the ministry can take place.

Issues for Further Exploration

It is the quest for the visible unity of the church which has led the Faith and Order Commission to produce the BEM document. The assumption is that agreement among the churches on issues which are keeping them divided will enable them to unite. The document itself challenges the churches to make deliberate efforts to overcome their divisions. The section on baptism affirms that our one baptism into Christ constitutes a call to the churches to overcome their divisions and visibly manifest their fellowship (Par. 6), but our experience is that reaching agreement on theological and other issues does not necessarily lead to visible unity. The Methodist Church in India did not come into the Church of North India, even though it had been a party to the agreements arrived at earlier. The C.S.I.-Lutheran plan for the formation of a united church has made little progress since 1967, even though agreements had been reached, and no further questions have been raised by any of the churches. Other examples could be given.

One problem seems to be the attachment of churches to a certain experience of their selfhood and identity and a feeling of insecurity and fear they face when they are called upon to enter into the new selfhood and identity of a united church, however richer the new identity may be. Such fear and hesitation have been evident in relation to the adoption of a common name for the one church in which the C.N.I., the C.S.I., and the Mar Thoma Church have affirmed that they belong together through the formation of the Joint Council. There is reluctance to give up the identity those churches have had, as well as the name representing their selfhood and identity. In the discussions about organic union among churches, the figure of death and resurrection has often been helpful. Each uniting church dies to the older self-identity and rises with Christ to a new identity. This is not always easy for churches to go through. The situation, however, challenges us to pursue more deeply the question of the nature of the visible unity of the church to which we are called.

One question to be raised is whether the goal of visible unity can be identified with the establishment of new ecclesiastical structures which replace existing structures. The oneness of the disciples for which Christ prayed was one which would enable the world to believe that Christ was sent by God. This certainly implies that the unity for which Christ prayed and which the church is called to manifest has power and vitality to challenge the world to believe. What is the essential ecclesial reality underlying the ecclesiastical structures?

In pursuing this question we must take seriously the relationship between Christology and ecclesiology. Even though reference to a christological method for Faith and Order had been made earlier, it was at the Lund conference on Faith and Order that an explicit suggestion of the relation between Christology and ecclesiology was made by T. F. Torrance and others. The new Faith and Order methodology adopted following the Lund conference, replacing the earlier comparative methodology, has also been described as the christological method. There is a good critical description of this methodology in a recent study by Kucheria Pathil, an Indian Roman Catholic theologian.[8]

The key to this method is the recognition that the quest for the ecclesial reality is integrally related to the quest for the reality of Christ. The basic question is how we discern, witness to, and manifest the reality of Christ so that the world today may believe in him. In the manner in which the BEM document has formulated the interpretation of baptism, eucharist, and ministry, it is clear that it is in the reality of Christ that the church has its being. It is life in Christ which the members of the church experience through the Holy Spirit. It is Christ's ministry which the church is called to fulfill. For the discernment of Christ the apostolic testimony to the ministry of Jesus is the key. What does the testimony that the Risen Lord wanted his disciples to meet him in Galilee mean? Does it not mean that the Risen Lord continues the ministry begun in Galilee? It is significant that in the gospel accounts a major part is devoted to Jesus' ministry among the sick, the needy, and the marginalized. He is described as making people whole, rehumanizing those who had been dehumanized by sin and evil structures. In such a ministry were seen signs of the reign of God. Discernment of the presence of such signs today is important for identifying the relation between Christology and ecclesiology.

In Asia there is a concern today to evaluate the role of action groups involved in justice struggles, many of whom are inspired by the gospel of Jesus

---

[8]*Models in Ecumenical Dialogue* (Bangalore: Dharmaram Publications, 1981), chap. 7.

Christ but are unrelated to traditional church life. In recent discussions in Asia the question of their ecclesial character has been raised without arriving at any conclusions. Some would regard them as outside the scope of the church, while others would like to bring them into the fellowship of the church. The real question is the manner in which the ecclesial reality is to be expressed in the world today if it is to witness to Christ who came as Jesus of Nazareth.

Finally, there are two other related questions, one about the meaning and practice of baptism, the other about the eucharist.

With regard to baptism, the dimension of commitment to corporateness of the community has already been referred to. However, the fact remains that it is individual persons who are baptized and made members of the community. The significance of this practice needs to be probed more deeply. Does the Christian mission require that all have to be baptized? Is baptism the necessary and only means of incorporation of people into the Body of Christ? In Asia the concept of baptism as requiring people to leave their religious and cultural heritage and join the church as a new religious community has been offensive to many. Many have felt that it was not essential for their faith response to Christ that they should receive baptism and thus cut themselves off from their cultural heritage. Two great converts in India, Brahmabandhav Upadhyaya (1861-1907) and Manilal Parekh (1885-1967), even though they had been baptized, wanted to describe themselves as Hindu Christians. Their concern was that when a person became a Christian he or she should not have to cease to be a Hindu.

In this connection we also need to ask what the significance is of the great commission in Mt. 28:18-20 about the baptism of *nations*. In Mt. 25:31-46, the parable of the final judgment, it is *nations* which are judged rather than individuals. Does this mean that, even though the church is to continue to baptize individuals, the goal is the conversion and transformation of corporate structures such as nations and communities? The question of whether only the baptized belong to the fellowship of the Body of Christ should also be considered, bearing in mind the fact that there are communities such as the Salvation Army, the Quakers, and the Subba Rao Christians in India who do not have the sacrament of baptism and yet claim to belong to Christ. The more radical and controversial concept of anonymous Christians of Karl Rahner also deserves to be considered for a deeper understanding of baptism and the church's oneness and mission.

With regard to the eucharist, the meaning of the real presence of Christ needs deeper reflection. The concept itself has a long history which makes it difficult. The presence of Christ in the eucharist is certainly a deep mystery which cannot be formulated in simple, rational terms. Yet it is important to raise questions which will safeguard the sacrament from being taken for granted as a means of saving grace. One important question to be probed is the meaning of "do this" in the words of Jesus at the last supper. If we read the passages carefully, it is clear that they do not mean simply eating and drinking. It is meant to be something which proclaims the death of our Lord till he comes again (1 Cor. 11:26). Does it not mean that the self-giving of Christ symbolized by the broken bread and the wine is to be continued in the life and witness of the church? It is through the continuance of the suffering and death of Christ in the life of the church that the saving death of Christ is made known. It is also through such experience that the church knows the power of the resurrection.

Another question is about the location of the real presence of Christ. Traditionally, it is associated with the eucharistic service itself and the elements, but the eucharistic service is also meant to enable the members to be involved in the mission of Christ in the world. The real presence is to be sought and manifested in the situations where the reconciling ministry of Christ overcoming the powers of evil is to be fulfilled. Does this not suggest a dialectic movement from a sacramental experience of Christ to a real experience of Christ? There are two levels of real presence of Christ: one in the sacrament, and the other in the situation of life in the world. The two are related to each other. If the sacramental experience does not lead to the real experience in the world, it may become irrelevant. At the same time, without the sacramental experience the quest for experience in the world may become a purely humanitarian exercise without the power of God.

BEM RECEPTION AND THE CONCERNS OF WOMEN IN THE THIRD WORLD

Victoria Chandran

I am pleased to have a part in this BEM reception program, even though I am not a professional theologian. What I have to say is in light of my experiences of involvement with women's struggles in the Church of South India, particularly reflecting on the document from the point of view of Third World women. My comments are primarily relevant to India, although from some of the women's conferences I have attended I understand that situations are more or less similar in Sri Lanka and in Madagascar and other African countries.

One of the distinctive characteristics of the Christian faith from the beginning is that the gospel which is the good news of Jesus Christ is to be shared with others. It is this commission which has made the Christian faith a missionary religion. Baptism is an integral part of the great commission, and, throughout the world, in almost every denomination it is the sacrament administered as a symbol of the new covenant between God and humankind. The BEM document makes tremendous affirmations about the gospel in what is said about baptism, eucharist, and ministry. For example: "Baptism has a dynamic which embraces the whole of life, extends to all nations" (Baptism, Par. 7). "Through baptism, Christians are brought into union with Christ, with each other and with the Church of every time and place" (Baptism, Par. 6).

Against such bold affirmations about the church and its mission, we should look at the realities of the world, particularly the Third World. These realities are similar to what Jesus sought to transform through his ministry. The poor, the weak, the sick, and the downtrodden became his concern. Loving one's neighbor for whatever he or she is, thereby establishing human solidarity, is good news. Baptism is not just to make people Christian but to make them fully human. The mission of the church is not simply to increase the numerical strength of the church but so to change the lives and attitudes of people that the quality of life for *all* people will be transformed. Only then does the gospel of Jesus Christ become good news for all.

Victoria M. Chandran (Church of South India) is a retired principal of the Bishop Cotton Girls' High School in Bangalore, India, and also served as a high school teacher and principal of two training schools for many years. She has long been active in the Women's Fellowship of the Church of South India, including being the keynote speaker at two of their quadrennial conferences. She is a past chairperson of the board of the Women's Fellowship motherhouse in Bangalore, and has been involved in the women's organization of the Christian Peace Conference, taking part in C. P. C. meetings in Finland and Czechoslovakia. She holds a B.A. and an L.T. (licentiate in teaching) from the University of Madras and had a year of special studies in Christian education at the Divinity School of the University of Chicago in 1957-58. While accompanying her husband as a visiting professor in the U.S.A. during 1983-84, she has taken part in many ecumenical gatherings in addition to the Hyde Park BEM Reception conference.

In India alone, more than 300,000,000 people live below the poverty line. Along with such poverty there are also people living in great affluence, enjoying all the benefits of the modern scientific and technological age. In this context the lot of women is far worse than that of men. This is true in both church and society. In some ways society in India, because of its secular constitution, is ahead of the church in dealing with the rights of women. Even in society, however, women are far behind men in many areas such as literacy, employment, health (due to malnutrition, since a woman always has to eat *after* her husband and others), constant childbirth, etc. Discrimination against women has also been observed in the applications of laws relating to rape, prostitution, dowry, inheritance, and the like.

If we take seriously the affirmation of the BEM document, the church through the sacraments of baptism and eucharist and through its ministry is to witness to the power of Christ, uniting all people within one fellowship and removing all barriers of injustice. I would especially point to the witness of the church in giving women their rightful dignity. In India, and perhaps in other areas too, women constitute the majority of churchgoers. They are the fundraisers of the church. In our country, in the fields of medicine and education they have played and are playing leading roles. What is known as the "least coin" fund was started by an Indian woman—Shanti Solomon of the Church of North India. The rehabilitation of the widows was started by a woman—Pandita Ramabai. Dr. B. V. Subamma of the Lutheran Church in India has pioneered rural evangelism. In India there is an association of theologically trained women who meet regularly to express their concern both for the life and mission of the church and for a more responsible share for women in the total ministry of the church. Women behind the purdah had been evangelized by the Church of England Zenana Mission women. But, when it comes to decision-making bodies in the church, women's place is not recognized.

Women in the Church of South India constitute "the silent majority." At the C.S.I. Synod of 1974, a decision was made that wherever *possible* women should have a thirty-percent representation on all committees and councils. This has not been implemented at either the diocesan or the synod level. In the Karnataka Central Diocese there is one woman on the Executive Committee. In most of the dioceses there are none. While the C.S.I. and the C.N.I. have agreed to ordain women, no woman has been ordained as presbyter yet, although many have graduated from theological colleges.

Many wrong interpretations in the church about "the true nature of women," "her intrinsic gifts," "the mission given by Christ," and the like have kept women down. The church has accepted the ancient Hebrew tradition as God's plan for all time. The Indian Church unfortunately has added the Indian culture and tradition to the Judeo-Greek tradition to keep women "in their proper place." This is true in most developing countries where women play an inferior role culturally. While outside the church in the secular world tremendous changes are taking place for the emancipation of women, in the churches women have been conditioned to accept a "mutilated existence" as normal. The BEM document affirms, "Where Christ is present, human barriers are being broken. The Church is called to convey to the world the image of a new humanity. There is in Christ no male or female" (Ministry, Par. 18).

One of the arguments given by many church leaders in India—males, of course—against equality of status for women in the total life of the church, including the ordained ministry, is that it is not in accordance with Indian culture. Here we should ask whether the gospel of Jesus Christ comes only to keep us in conformity with the culture or to transform it. To quote BEM, "Those baptized are called upon to reflect the glory of the Lord as they are transformed by the power of the Holy Spirit" (Baptism, Par. 9). Our faith as elaborated in the BEM document is that we are not able to live in conformity with the world. Our witness is to the transforming power of the gospel. None of the reasons given to bar women from playing an effective role in the church can be maintained. By denying women their rightful place, the church is denying the worth and dignity which God intended for them, which is the very denial of salvation itself.

In India, where the church is a tiny minority, its fellowship has often been broken by jealousies, ambitions, and wrong attitudes toward women. Men have dominated the leadership of committees at all levels. Barriers of all kinds have been erected to maintain the status quo. If we confess Jesus Christ as the life of the world, we have to accept the concept of universality or, as the BEM document puts it, "A new humanity in which barriers of division . . . are transcended" (Baptism, Par. 2). All persons belong to the same family. If we do not realize this, we do not understand the sovereignty of God, and our confession of Christ will become like those clubs which say "For Men Only."

God's love is for all people. Christ's ministry, death, and resurrection brought about a new relationship between human beings. A new community was called. The BEM document states: "In a broken world God calls the whole of humanity to become God's people" (Ministry, Par. 1). Again, "The word *ministry* in its broadest sense denotes the service to which the whole people of God is called" (Ministry, Par. 7b). "In order to fulfill this mission faithfully, they will seek relevant forms of witness and service in each situation. In so doing they bring to the world a foretaste of the joy and glory of God's Kingdom" (Ministry, Par. 4). Thus, ministry and service belong to the *whole people of God*. The call to ministry and service comes to all—both male and female.

I stress this point because of my conviction that one area where the church has to recapture the revolutionary freedom of the gospel is the responsible participation of men and women in the human community. The church should follow the liberation offered by the style of Jesus of Nazareth. Hierarchical structures, doctrinal teachings, and constitutional regulations should be transformed to make women equal partners with men. Male and female were created in God's image, and there is one God for all. Christ's death on the cross liberated both men and women. By conveying the message of the resurrection through a woman, Christ fulfilled this liberation. "As participants in the eucharist . . . we prove inconsistent if we are not actively participating in [the] ongoing restoration of the world's situation and the human condition. . . . we are placed under continual judgment by persistence of unjust relationships of all kinds in our society" (Eucharist, Par. 20).

This challenging affirmation of the BEM document must open our eyes to all areas of the church where injustices are practiced. It is not enough to proclaim equality, justice, and human rights from the pulpit while keeping the majority of God's people down. These should be practiced within the church to make the proclamation effective. As the document so effectively puts it, "The sharing in one bread and the common cup . . . demonstrates and effects the oneness of sharers with Christ" (Eucharist, Par. 19).

I conclude with a statement from a preparatory paper for one of the Vancouver issue groups, written by Cynthia Wedel, past co-president of the World Council of Churches:

> If we believe that God is a remote first cause who set the creation in motion and laid down the rules in the Bible for all time, we need not justify change—such as the role of women in church and ministry. But if we believe in a God living, acting, and making all things new —a God who finds many ways to open new insights and possibilities to humankind—then the changing role of women can be affirmed as God's leading us into new ways of human relationships.

"BAPTISM, EUCHARIST, AND MINISTRY"
—AND RECEPTION

William G. Rusch

The Pre-History of BEM

A long and prolonged history lies behind the light gray and green volume now circulating in some eleven or twelve languages and known as BEM. The story has been often told, in a convenient form in the two-volume *A History of the Ecumenical Movement.*[1]

The first thoughts of a world conference on Faith and Order are rightly associated with the World Missionary Conference, Edinburgh, 1910. Bishop Charles Brent and Robert Gardiner, both of the Episcopal Church, believed that the time had come in 1910 to examine matters of faith and order in a world conference—items which had been excluded from the Edinburgh program. Activities began almost immediately and continued up to the outbreak of World War I. After the war they continued, and, in August, 1927, the first World Conference of Faith and Order assembled at Lausanne. It is still worthwhile to examine the Proceedings of this conference. The continuity of Faith and Order work for over fifty years is obvious. It is true that the notes to the final report are but a listing of differing viewpoints concerning the nature of unity, but the closing report,

---

[1]Ruth Rouse and Stephen Charles Neill, eds., *A History of the Ecumenical Movement, 1517-1948,* 2nd ed. (Philadelphia: Westminster Press, 1967); Howard E. Fey, ed., *A History of the Ecumenical Movement, 1948-1968* (Philadelphia: Westminster Press, 1970).

William Graham Rusch (Lutheran Church in America) has been Director for Ecumenical Relations, Division for World Mission and Ecumenism, of the Lutheran Church in America since 1979. He was also Adjunct Professor of Historical Theology at the General Theological Seminary, New York, 1978-82. He was previously Associate Executive Director of the Division of Theological Studies, Lutheran Council in the U.S.A., 1971-78, and Director of Fortress Press, 1978-79. After his 1966 ordination, he served a church in New York City, then chaired the Classical Languages Dept. at Augsburg College, Minneapolis. He holds a B.A. and an M.A. from the State University of New York at Buffalo, a B.D. from the Lutheran Theological Seminary at Philadelphia, and a Ph.D. from the Theology Faculty of the University of Oxford, Mansfield College (1965), with further study at the Universities of Pennsylvania and Minnesota. Dr. Rusch was a member of the U.S.A. Lutheran-Roman Catholic Dialogue (1971-78) and of the Advisory Committee of the Office of Jewish-Christian Relations of the National Council of Churches (1972-81). He has been on the N.C.C. Governing Board since 1979; a member of the W.C.C. Commission of Faith and Order since 1980; and Vice President of the N.C.C., as chair of its F. and O. Commission (1982-85), having been a member of F. and O. since 1972. His articles have appeared in several scholarly journals, and he has been a series editor for Sources of Early Christian Thought (Fortress Press), which will publish his *The Liturgical Life of the Early Church* as vol. 8. Also forthcoming are an English edition of P. Nauten's *Origen* (Fortress) and a life of Athanasius of Alexandria.

129

The Call to Unity, which was unanimously adopted, reveals both the consistency of the ecumenical movement and its rate of speed:

> God wills unity. Our presence in this conference bears testimony to our desire to bend our wills to His . . . God's Spirit has been in the midst of us . . . His presence has been manifest in our worship, our deliberations and our fellowship . . . We can never be the same again.
>
> Some of us, pioneers in this undertaking, have grown old in our search for unity. It is to youth that we look to lift the torch on high. We men have carried too much alone through many years. The women henceforth should be accorded their share of responsibility. And so the whole Church will be enabled to do that which no section can hope to perform.[2]

This text was drafted in 1927! Lausanne finally adopted texts on the nature of the church, the church's common confession of faith, the ministry, and the sacraments. The journey had begun.

The Second World Conference on Faith and Order assembled in August, 1937, in Edinburgh. It marked a definite advance upon Lausanne. The goal is "to realize the idea of the Church as one living body, worshipping and serving God in Christ."[3] This would involve both an inner spiritual unity and that outward unity "which expresses itself in mutual recognition, cooperative action, and corporate or spiritual unity."[4] The goal of visible unity thus began to be asserted. Edinburgh's *Affirmation of Allegiance* took its place with Lausanne's *The Call to Unity*.

Another war again suspended ecumenical progress, but the World Council of Churches was formed in 1948 in Amsterdam. Faith and Order now became part of this larger entity. This First Assembly of the W.C.C. expressed the basis for the search for outward unity: "God has given to His people in Jesus Christ a unity which is His creation and not our achievement. We praise and thank Him for a mighty work of His Holy Spirit, by which we have been drawn together to discover that, notwithstanding our divisions, we are one in Jesus Christ."[5] This comes from the statement, *The Universal Church in God's Design*, which merits being read in its entirety if for no other reason than that its drafters were Karl Barth, Edmund Schlink, K. E. Skydsgaard, Georges Florovsky, and Douglas Horton.

The third World Conference of Faith and Order was held in Lund in August, 1952. Here the theme of "outward unity" introduced at Edinburgh and affirmed at Amsterdam was developed further:

---

[2]H. N. Bate, ed., *Faith and Order, Proceedings of the World Conference, Lausanne, August 3-21, 1927* (London: Student Christian Movement, 1927), pp. 460-461.

[3]Leonard Hodgson, ed., *The Second World Conference on Faith and Order Held at Edinburgh, August 3-18, 1937* (London: SCM Press, 1938), p. 250.

[4]Ibid., p. 259.

[5]W. A. Visser't Hooft, ed., *The First Assembly of the World Council of Churches* (London: SCM Press, 1949). p. 51.

> We are agreed that there are not two Churches, one visible and the other invisible, but one Church which must find visible expression on earth, but we differ in our understanding of the character of the unity of the Church on earth for which we hope . . . Yet our differences in the doctrinal and sacramental content of our faith and our hope do not prevent us from being one in the act of believing and of hoping.[6]

But if Lund marked a continuation in commitment to visible unity, it disclosed the end of the method of "comparative ecclesiology." As the report "A Word to the Churches" states on its first page,

> We have seen clearly that we can make no real advance towards unity if we only compare our several conceptions of the nature of the Church and the traditions in which they are embodied. But once again it has been proved true that as we seek to draw closer to Christ we come closer to one another. We need, therefore, to penetrate behind our divisions to a deeper and richer understanding of the mystery of the God-given union of Christ with his Church."[7]

Lund concluded: to get beyond the impasse of "comparative ecclesiology" the doctrine of the church needs to be treated in close relation both to the doctrine of Christ and to the doctrine of the Holy Spirit. In the "summary and prospect" section Lund declared that "the nature of the unity towards which we are striving is that of a visible fellowship in which all members, acknowledging Jesus Christ as living Lord and Saviour, shall recognize each other as belonging fully to His Body, to the end that the world may believe."[8]

The Second Assembly of the W.C.C. meeting in August, 1954, at Evanston developed the approach of the Lund conference by bringing Christology and eschatology together:

> Through the indwelling Spirit, the Comforter, who leads the Church in all truth, the unity of the Church even now is a foretaste of the fulness that is to be because it already is; therefore, the Church can work tirelessly and wait patiently and expectantly for the day when God shall sum up all things in Christ.[9]

> It is certain that the perfect unity of the Church will not be totally achieved until God sums up all things in Christ. But the New Testament affirms that this unity is already being realized within the present historical order. By the power of his resurrection, Christ has

---

[6] Oliver S. Tomkins, ed., *The Third World Conference on Faith and Order Held at Lund, August 15th to 28th, 1952* (London: SCM Press, 1953), pp. 33-34.

[7] Ibid., p. 15.

[8] Ibid., p. 37.

[9] W. A. Visser't Hooft, ed., *The Evanston Report: The Second Assembly of the World Council of Churches, 1954* (London: SCM Press, 1955), p. 84.

granted this grace to His Church even now, and the signs of His work
are discernible to him who has eyes to see. In the upheavals of the
present hour, Jesus Christ is gathering His people in a true community of faith and obedience without respect for existing divisions.[10]

Evanston expressed the commitment to unity christologically rooted; its view of
that goal was still less than clear: "In the World Council of Churches we still
intend to stay together. But beyond that, as the Holy Spirit may guide us, we
intend to unite."[11]

   The Fourth Assembly of the W.C.C. in New Delhi in November and December, 1961, developed more fully the concept of unity, affirming the model of
"organic unity." This model as the goal of ecumenism makes the commitment
to "one fully committed fellowship" of all Christians "in each place." The significant section, which has been compared in its complexity to a Pauline sentence,
reads:

> We believe that the unity which is both God's will and his gift to his
> church is being made visible as all in each place who are baptized into
> Jesus Christ and confess him as Lord and Saviour are brought by the
> Holy Spirit into one fully committed fellowship holding the one
> apostolic faith, preaching the one gospel, breaking the one bread,
> joining in common prayer, and having a corporate life reaching out
> in witness and service to all, and who at the same time are united
> with the whole Christian fellowship in all places and all ages in such
> wise that ministry and members are accepted by all, and that all can
> act and speak together as occasion requires for the tasks to which
> God calls his people.[12]

   Two years after the New Delhi Assembly, the Fourth World Conference on
Faith and Order met in July, 1963, in Montreal. This meeting was decisive in
its distinction between the Tradition of the gospel and various Christian traditions and in its articulation of the norms for evolving the apostolic character
and mutual recognition of ministers and ministries. The entire Montreal report
deserves attention before any judgment is made about BEM:

> In our present situation, we wish to reconsider the problem of Scrip-
> ture and Tradition, or rather that of Tradition and Scripture. And
> therefore we wish to propose the following statement as a fruitful
> way of reformulating the question. Our starting-point is that we are
> all living in a tradition which goes back to our Lord and has its roots
> in the Old Testament, and are all indebted to that tradition inas-
> much as we have received the revealed truth, the Gospel, through its
> being transmitted from one generation to another. Thus we can say

[10]Ibid., pp. 88-89.
[11]Ibid., p. 90.
[12]W. A. Visser't Hooft, ed., *The New Delhi Report: The Third Assembly of the World
Council of Churches, 1961* (London: SCM Press, 1962), p. 116.

that we exist as Christians by the Tradition of the Gospel (the *para-dosis* of the *kerygma*) testified in the Scripture, transmitted in and by the Church through the power of the Holy Spirit. Tradition taken in this sense is actualized in the preaching of the Word, in the administration of the Sacraments and worship, in Christian teaching and theology, and in mission and witness to Christ by the lives of the members of the Church.

What is transmitted in the process of tradition is the Christian faith, not only as a sum of tenets, but as a living reality transmitted through the operation of the Holy Spirit. We can speak of the Christian Tradition (with a capital T), whose content is God's revelation and self-giving in Christ, present in the life of the Church.

But this Tradition which is the work of the Holy Spirit is embodied in traditions (in the two senses of the word, both as referring to diversity in forms of expression, and in the sense of separate communions). The traditions in Christian history are distinct from, and yet connected with, the Tradition. They are the expressions and manifestations in diverse historical forms of the one truth and reality which is Christ.[13]

The Montreal conference asked: "Does not the ecumenical situation demand that we search for the Tradition by re-examining sincerely our own particular traditions?"[14] The great contribution of this Faith and Order conference was to highlight the critical distinction between the Tradition and different traditions of churches which transmit the Tradition in historically conditioned forms.

Meanwhile, criticisms were raised about the New Delhi statement on unity. While the unity of all in each place was spelled out, the relationship of those in one place was not. The catholicity of the church was noted, but its marks were not given. Some of these comments had been made at Montreal in 1963. The concerns were sharpened with the calling of the Second Vatican Council in 1962 and especially its "The Dogmatic Constitution on the Church," 1964.

As a result of these concerns the Fourth Assembly of the W.C.C., meeting in Uppsala in July, 1968, addressed the issue of catholicity, as excerpts from its report indicate:

Yet it is within this very world that God makes catholicity available to men through the ministry of Christ in his Church. The purpose of Christ is to bring people of all times, of all races, of all places, of all conditions, into an organic and living unity in Christ by the Holy Spirit under the universal fatherhood of God. This unity is not solely external; it has a deeper internal dimension, which is also expressed by the term "catholicity." Catholicity reaches its completion when

[13]P. C. Rodger and Lukas Vischer, eds., *The Fourth World Conference on Faith and Order, Montreal, 1963* (New York: Association Press, 1964), pp. 51-52.
[14]Ibid., p. 54.

what God has already begun in history is finally disclosed and fulfilled.[15]

Catholicity is a gift of the Spirit, but it is also a task, a call and
engagement.[16]

The Church is bold in speaking of itself as the sign of the coming
unity of humankind.[17]

The unity of man is grounded for the Christian not only in his creation by the one God in his own image, but in Jesus Christ who "for
us men" became man, was crucified, and who constitutes the Church
which is his body as a new community of new creatures. The catholicity of the Church means this given reality of grace in which the
purpose of creation is restored and sinful men are reconciled in the
one divine sonship of which Christ is both author and finisher.[18]

The paradigm of organic unity within catholicity received fuller treatment
at meetings of the Commission on Faith and Order in Louvain in 1971 and Sala-
manca in 1973. A new term entered the ecumenical vocabulary with "conciliar
fellowship." The Louvain report included these words:

Conciliarity has been, in some form or degree, characteristic of the
life of the Christian Church in all ages and at various levels. By conciliarity we mean the coming together of Christians—locally, regionally
or globally—for common prayer, counsel and decision, in the belief
that the Holy Spirit can use such meetings for his own purpose of
reconciling, reviewing and reforming the Church by guiding it towards the fulness of truth and love.[19]

In this model each "truly united" local church is an expression of organic unity
attained on the local level and has in conciliar fellowship with other organically
united local churches "the fulness of catholicity" and "the fulness of truth and
love." In this way each local church participates in the full conciliarity of the
entire church. However, conciliar fellowship is not to be an end in itself. It is
to make possible a genuinely ecumenical council that would allow all churches
to take part. Already in 1968 at Uppsala the goal of a council had been mentioned:

The ecumenical movement helps to enlarge this experience of universality, and its regional councils and its World Council may be regarded as a transitional opportunity for eventually actualizing a truly
universal, ecumenical, conciliar form of common life and witness.

[15]Norman Goodall, ed., *The Uppsala Report, 1968* (Geneva: World Council of Churches,
1968), p. 13.
[16]Ibid.
[17]Ibid., p. 17.
[18]Ibid., p. 18.
[19]*Faith and Order, Louvain, 1971.* Faith and Order Paper 59 (Geneva: World Council of
Churches, 1971), p. 226.

The members of the World Council of Churches, committed to each other, should work for the time when a genuinely universal council may once more speak for all Christians, and lead the way into the future.[20]

The Faith and Order Commission in Louvain spoke to the churches: "They [the churches] should be asked to consider both the question how far a true conciliarity marks their existing life and also the question whether their life and work are helping to prepare the way for a 'genuinely ecumenical Council.' "[21]

The Fifth Assembly of the W.C.C., meeting in Nairobi in November and December, 1975, brought together the strands of the story we have been tracing when it adopted a description of the unity to be realized in the ecumenical movement:

> The one Church is to be envisioned as a conciliar fellowship of local churches which are themselves truly united. In this conciliar fellowship each local church possesses, in communion with the others, the fulness of catholicity, witnesses to the same apostolic faith, and therefore recognizes the others as belonging to the same church of Christ and guided by the same Spirit. They are bound together because they have received the same doctrine, and share in the same eucharist; they recognize each other's members and ministries. They are one in their common commitment to confess the gospel of Christ by proclamation and service to the world. To this end, each church aims at maintaining sustained and sustaining relationships with her sister churches in conciliar gatherings whenever required for the fulfilment of their common calling. . . .

> It [conciliar fellowship] does *not* look towards a conception of unity different from that full organic unity sketched in the New Delhi Statement, but is rather a further elaboration of it. The term is intended to describe an aspect of the life of the one undivided Church at *all* levels. In the first place, it expresses the unity of churches separated by distance, culture, and time, a unity which is publicly manifested when the representatives of these local churches gather together for a common meeting. It also refers to a quality of life within each local church; it underlies the fact that true unity is not monolithic, does not overreach the special gifts given to each member and to each local church, but rather cherishes and protects them.[22]

In 1978 the meeting of the Faith and Order Commission in Bangalore was able to advance the report of Nairobi, "What Unity Requires," by identifying

[20]Goodall, *Uppsala Report*, p. 17.
[21]*Faith and Order, Louvain, 1971*, p. 228.
[22]David M. Paton, ed., *Breaking Barriers, Nairobi, 1975* (London: SPCK; Grand Rapids: Wm. B. Eerdmans, 1976), p. 60.

the three elements of conciliar fellowship needed for a reunited church; (1) a common understanding of the apostolic faith; (2) full mutual recognition of baptism, eucharist, and ministry; and (3) agreement on common ways of teaching and decision-making.[23] If the churches are ultimately able to make a positive official response to BEM, one of these three requirements for calling a truly universal council will have been met. This is the challenge and excitement of BEM.

We have traced the history and shaping of the goal of unity in conciliar ecumenism that have called forth BEM. We must now see how this document came into being.

Der Urtext of BEM: "One Baptism, One Eucharist, and a Mutually Recognized Ministry"

As the preceding section has indicated, conciliar ecumenism, a quest for the visible unity of the church, has always involved theological discussion of baptism and eucharist. Between Lund in 1952 and Montreal in 1963, baptism was a major concern.[24] Study continued to find common perspectives on baptism and eucharist. Roman Catholic theologians entered the debate. Baptism was considered at Bristol in 1967 at the Faith and Order Commission meeting and in 1969 at Reunice, CSSR. The results of the study, *Baptism, Confirmation, and Eucharist*, were submitted to the meeting at Louvain in 1971.

The eucharist was also discussed at Bristol in 1967. The Fourth Assembly in Uppsala in 1968 requested study of intercommunion. In 1969 the report, "Beyond Intercommunion," was published. As all these studies developed, the proposal was made to bring together in two documents the agreements on baptism and the eucharist which had been reached in the ecumenical movement. In Louvain in 1971 two statements, "Ecumenical Agreement on Baptism" and "The Eucharist in Ecumenical Thought," were presented for discussion. These reports were brought to the meeting of the Faith and Order Commission in Accra in 1974.

With regard to ministry the situation was somewhat different. Already at Lausanne in 1927 and Edinburgh in 1937 the question of the ordained ministry played an important role. It was recognized that a ministry acknowledged in every part of the church as possessing the sanction of the whole church was needed. The debate revealed apparently insurmountable differences on the authority and function of the ministry. There was so little hope for progress

---

[23]*Faith and Order, Minutes, Bangalore, 1978* (Geneva: World Council of Churches, 1979).

[24]See *One Lord, One Baptism: Report on the Divine Trinity and the Unity of the Church and Report on the Meaning of Baptism by the Theological Commission on Christ and the Church*. Faith and Order Paper 29 (London: SCM Press, 1960); and Rodger and Vischer, *The Fourth World Conference*.

that attempts were dropped to study the ministry as a separate subject. Only in 1963 at Montreal did it again become part of the agenda. In the interval new studies had occurred in New Testament and patristic research. Much of this scholarship was across confessional traditions. New appreciation of the relationship of ordained ministry to the priesthood of all believers was one result of this study. Thus, a study on ministry was undertaken by Faith and Order after Montreal. A report, "The Ordained Ministry," was shared at Louvain. Consultations were held in Marseilles in 1972 and Geneva in 1973.

In 1974 the Faith and Order Commission meeting in Accra received all this material on the three topics and produced three agreed statements. The commission stated that it was surprised by the degree of mutual understanding and recommended that the texts be published for information and the response of theologians and others. The result is *Der Urtext of BEM, One Baptism, One Eucharist, and a Mutually Recognized Ministry*. Authorized for distribution by the Central Committee meeting in West Berlin and the Nairobi Assembly in 1975, it was published as Faith and Order Paper 73 with the subtitle, "Three Agreed Statements." This statement and its introduction by Lukas Vischer are worth the attention of anyone who wishes to see BEM in its historical developments. The *Urtext* is *three* reports. The churches were requested to consider and comment on it. The preface makes clear that visible unity will not be achieved without agreement on these topics. It is pointed out that theologians of widely different traditions worked on these texts, including for some years now Roman Catholics. The contribution of dialogues is noted as well as changes that have occurred in the churches themselves. The churches have reexamined traditional convictions and practices in the light of liturgical revival and common biblical studies. New fellowships have arisen across denominational lines.

The special character of the three reports needs to be stressed. They did not represent a consensus but a summary of shared convictions and perspectives. Their purpose was to help bring churches closer together, to make possible a mutual recognition. They are not a complete theological treatment of baptism, eucharist, and ministry. The reports deal with those aspects of these themes which are directly or indirectly related to mutual recognition. The language is classical theological language. This is inevitable. But the preface declares that these reports are not the last word. Finally, they must be translated into the languages of our time. The churches are advised that, if they are to live together in unity, they will have to accept and develop insights which are either new to them or which they have not emphasized in their particular tradition. "Many may be tempted to examine them [the three reports] to see if what is said in them does full justice to the distinctiveness of their own tradition." The reports try to answer how the churches are ever "to establish together a fellowship of mutual recognition." The Faith and Order Commission requested responses from the churches, including what changes and renewal in doctrine, liturgy, and practice would be required in each church.

When we turn to BEM itself, the similarities and differences between the

Urtext and BEM will become apparent. The *Urtext* has set the form for BEM, but there are many differences to note. I note just two now: The *Urtext* is really three texts, not one, and the responses requested from the churches to the *Urtext* and BEM are to be quite different. The great commonality they share is the purpose of advancing the visible unity of the church. A detailed analysis of the two documents is not possible within the confines of this essay. Such an examination would disclose the remarkable advances in the work of Faith and Order and the entire ecumenical scene between 1974 and 1982.

The Lima Meeting of the Faith and Order Commission, January, 1982

After the Accra meeting in 1974, the Faith and Order Commission continued to work on the three topics of baptism, eucharist, and ministry. A steering committee under the leadership of Brother Max Thurian of Taizé began its work. Over 100 responses from practically every area of the world and every ecclesiastical tradition were received. These were carefully analyzed at a consultation in 1977. A special consultation on infant and believers' baptism was held in Louisville in 1978. All this material was discussed and reviewed at the Commission of Faith and Order meeting in Bangalore in 1978. In 1979 a special consultation met in Geneva on the question of *episkope* and the episcopate. The draft text of 1979 was the subject of a consultation for Orthodox theologians in the same year.

A draft text based on all this discussion, and more, was prepared for the meeting of the Faith and Order Commission in Lima in 1982. At Lima, plenary time was made available for major issues of substance. Details of style, small points, were referred to an editorial committee. In the course of the Lima meeting, 190 proposed revisions were considered. On January 12th the following motion was put before the Commission:

> The Commission considers the revised text on Baptism, Eucharist and Ministry to have been brought to such a stage of maturity that it is now ready for transmission to the churches in accordance with the mandate given at the Fifth Assembly of the World Council of Churches, Nairobi 1975, and re-affirmed by the Central Committee, Dresden 1981.[25]

The vote was taken on the one document, not on each section. The motion passed unanimously, without negative votes or abstentions. Over 100 theologians voted together—Roman Catholic, Orthodox, Lutheran, Anglican, and others. An

[25]Michael Kinnamon, ed., *Towards Visible Unity, Commission on Faith and Order, Lima, 1982*, vol. 1. Faith and Order Paper 112 (Geneva: World Council of Churches, 1982), pp. 83-84.

ecumenical milestone toward fulfilling one of the requirements for a universal council had been sent to the churches. The final text of BEM as revised in Lima was published as Faith and Order Paper 111 in the course of 1982 and made available in nearly a dozen languages.

The BEM Document and Its Continuing Challenge

Having traced the long history of the evolution of BEM, we must address the document itself. Some of the questions about the document can be answered more briefly in light of this historical sketch.

What is BEM? It is the product of over fifty-five years of the ecumenical movement in its conciliar form. As the By-Laws of the World Council of Churches state, "The Faith and Order Commission is to proclaim the oneness of the Church of Jesus Christ and to call the churches to the goal of visible unity in one faith and one eucharistic fellowship, expressed in worship and common life in Christ, in order that the world might believe." If divided churches are to achieve visible unity, one prerequisite is a basic agreement on baptism, eucharist, and ministry.

While BEM claims a remarkable degree of agreement, it does not claim the consensus that is necessary for visible unity. However, it does create an ecumenical vocabulary. Behind BEM is the recognition that, toward the goal of visible unity, churches will pass through stages marked by the identification of convergences. These convergences assure that, despite much diversity in theological expression, the churches have much in common in their understanding of the faith. BEM aims to become part of the faithful reflection of the common Christian tradition, the tradition of the gospel. Here we see the crucial influence of the Montreal meeting of 1963. Like *One Baptism, One Eucharist, and a Mutually Recognized Ministry*, BEM does not claim to be a complete theological treatment, nor does it claim to demonstrate major areas of theological convergence. It is to be evaluated in terms of the norms of the apostolic tradition, not in terms of later confessional, contextual, and polemical formulations. Unless it is remembered that the goal of BEM is to advance toward the mutual recognition of baptism, eucharist, and ministers and ministries, BEM is vulnerable to being misunderstood. A key question behind BEM is how much is unified or binding dogma in the tradition and how much is diversified or nonbinding theology. BEM is *sui generis*. That theologians of such widely different traditions should be able to speak so harmoniously about baptism, eucharist, and ministry is unprecedented, certainly, in the modern ecumenical movement, but we must remember that BEM concentrates on those aspects of the themes that directly or indirectly relate to the problems of mutual recognition leading to unity (see Preface, p. ix).

The Commission on Faith and Order at Lima did not approve the text. This distinction is important. It transmitted the text to the churches because, in the opinion of Faith and Order, it had reached a sufficient level of maturity. Unlike the *Urtext*, here the churches are not asked for comments. The churches are asked to take up the question of "reception" involving the whole people of God and all levels of church life. The churches are also asked to prepare an official response to the whole document at the highest level of authority. Faith and Order, unlike in 1974, voted on one coherent text. The question BEM poses to all Christians is not whether we find our denominational confessions in it but rather whether we find in BEM "the faith of the Church throughout the ages," or the *paradosis* of the *kerygma*. And, if we do, what does this mean?

Let us observe what BEM is asking of the churches. First is the question of reception:

> As concrete evidence of their ecumenical commitment, the churches are being asked to enable the widest possible involvement of the whole people of God at all levels of church life in the spiritual process of receiving this text.

Second is the issue of official response:

> The Faith and Order Commission now respectfully invites all churches to prepare an official response to this text at the highest appropriate level of authority, whether it be a council, synod, conference, assembly or other body. In support of this process of reception, the Commission would be pleased to know as precisely as possible.
> - the extent to which your church can recognize in this text the faith of the Church through the ages;
> - the consequences your church can draw from this text for its relations and dialogue with other churches, particularly with those churches which also recognize the text as an expression of the apostolic faith;
> - the guidance your church can take from this text for its worship, educational, ethical, and spiritual life and witness;
> - the suggestions your church can make for the ongoing work of Faith and Order as it relates the material of this text on Baptism, Eucharist and Ministry to its long-range research project, "Towards the Common Expression of the Apostolic Faith Today."[26]

This brings us to one of the most challenging and critical topics on the present ecumenical agenda—reception.

The Reception of BEM

I define "reception" to include all the phases and aspects of a process by which a church makes the result of a bilateral or multilateral conversation a part of its faith and life. In proposing this definition, I am not in conflict with the

---

[26]*Baptism, Eucharist, and Ministry*. Faith and Order Paper 111 (Geneva: World Council of Churches, 1982), p. x.

way it is being explained in most recent ecumenical documents. For example, Faith and Order Paper 91, "How Does the Church Teach Authoritatively Today?" states:

> In many churches there is today a stronger emphasis on the need for reception of teaching by the whole Church. . . . To the degree in which teaching has been arrived at through the participation of the entire body of Christ, reception will be facilitated. . . . The term "reception" must not be taken to imply that decisions are arranged "from above" and then simply submitted to the community for passive "reception." Reception is not only official endorsement, but also a profound appropriation (*Aneignung*) through a gradual testing process (*Bewahrung*) by which the teaching is digested into the life and liturgy of the community. . . . The Church's teaching will be authenticated by the blessings of the Spirit, not by the manifestation of Spirit and power!"[27]

The Third Forum on Bilateral Conversation devoted part of its discussion to reception.[28] While the discussion was centered around dialogues, the comments about reception have relevance for BEM:

> There are different levels of reception, different forms of reception and different ways of dealing with joint statements. Some of the texts and insights which result from bilateral or multilateral work stand on their own; they become a part of the faith consciousness of the Church without formal reception. Some of the documents, arising from dialogues, elicit an intensive discussion at all levels, including the church authorities; for many of these it is only possible, in retrospect, to say if they constituted an agreement in faith or were merely an intermediate step towards this. There are also texts that are written primarily for theologians, and still others which are written primarily for theologians, and still others which are intended to address the whole people of God. Reception has to be described in a different way for each of these examples. . . . Reception, in both its strict and comprehensive meanings, occurs only as Christ graciously accomplishes it by his Spirit.[29]

If the entire discussion of reception is novel, it is because we are in a new situation created in reference to BEM where there is now claimed convergence in those areas where for centuries there has been radical division. The churches are not just asked to approve three texts in one statement which may be considered legitimate statements about the theology and practice of baptism, eucharist, and ministry. They are also requested to have their faith and life touched at their

---

[27]*How Does the Church Teach Authoritatively Today?* Faith and Order Paper 91 (Geneva: World Council of Churches, 1979), p. 88.
[28]*The Third Forum on Bilateral Conversations.* Faith and Order Paper 107 (Geneva: World Council of Churches, 1982), pp. 38-44.
[29]Ibid., pp. 38-39.

deepest levels. The churches are being asked to accept and make their own something that they did not produce alone, or with one other tradition. This document comes in a sense from outside all of them, and its claims are bigger than
any one of them. Is it any wonder that reception has been seen as the main
future problem of the ecumenical movement?

Reception is also a much more complex phenomenon than some have suggested. It has several aspects. The competent and official authorities of the church
are involved, but so are the worship and life of the congregation. Contrary to
some views, reception will have to be more than a purely administrative or intellectual step. All concerned will have to see that the apostolicity and catholicity
of the church are intimately associated with what should be received. In this
process of reception, theologians can help, and they certainly should be salutary,
but the churches have the final word. When *One Baptism, One Eucharist, and
a Mutually Recognized Ministry* was issued, over 100 churches responded. That
process disclosed that something new had appeared on the ecumenical horizon.
While it was not reception, I would say that it was a harbinger of reception.

BEM is setting a problem before all the churches because it is claiming to
confront each church with the apostolic church. If no church today is willing
to claim that the way it practices baptism, eucharist, and ministry is completely
in conformity with the apostolic heritage, BEM is asking the churches what they
are prepared to do about this for the greater visible unity of the church. As I
have observed above, Faith and Order worked with comparative ecclesiology.
The method had its merits, but Lund in 1952 reached the end of those merits.
Lund represented a shift to the approach to formulate together the common
ground that can be affirmed by churches in union. The question of BEM is: Can
the convergence achieved by theologians be translated into the real life of each
church? This attempt at "translation" is part of the newness of BEM. After
centuries of excommunications and anathemas, we are now beginning the period
that holds the promise of synthesis, convergence, and openness.

Yet, it is a promise replete with danger. Reception could produce new
tensions and divisions, for what is involved here is something new and inescap-
able, which is a difficult step. Not all churches will find it easy to submit to the
reception process. It will force them to face the apostolic church. This is the
frame of reference of BEM. The celebration of baptism is the celebration of the
faith of the apostolic church. The celebration of the eucharist is the full display
of this apostolic faith in thanksgiving. Within the ecclesial community, ordained
ministry represents the indispensible reference of the ecclesial community to the
faith of the apostolic community and to the work of unifying and building up
the people of God, built on the foundation of the apostles and prophets.

I believe history will prove that the reception of BEM is not one case among
many. For all churches, BEM could be the test case. Reception of this document will have repercussions on the attitude of each church toward ecumenical
dialogue, the entire ecumenical movement, and in all areas of church life, including the ethical and social. If BEM is taken seriously, there is only one place for

the act of its reception, and that is the deepest level of the life of the church, where the church lives out the proclamation of the Word and the celebration of the sacraments. That is why BEM cannot be sent only to theological faculties. Rather, reception must be a work of the entire community of building up that whole community of love. Reception will, for a variety of reasons, move at differing rates. *Koinonia* among the churches will come by degree. Not all churches receiving BEM and the later convergence documents on the apostolic faith will at the same time find again the fullness of *koinonia*, but, by their reception, an essential ecclesiality will be reached.

If the Lutherans, using my own tradition as an example, are going to receive BEM, what will be needed is a new awareness of the demands of the faith received from the apostles and an openness and receptivity to evangelical values to which our tradition has so far shown less sensitivity. As Dom Emmanuel Lanne, a Benedictine from Belgium, stated at Lima, "It is essential that all the churches should see that the reception of BEM concerns them at the center of their being. What is at stake here is the full communion which they desire to recover and the visible unity to which they are called."[30] I cannot predict how Lutherans will react to BEM, and I suspect nationally and internationally there will not be *one* Lutheran response to the challenge of the reception of BEM. Like many other churches, Lutheran churches will be confronted here by the question of teaching authority in the church. Where is it? How does it function? They will encounter a new, or at least different, vocabulary. They will feel challenges at some of their most cherished points. Yet, I believe that we have resources within the Lutheran tradition to take BEM seriously and, when we do, we become not less confessional Lutherans, but precisely more confessional.

BEM asks of us all as confessions to affirm the sacraments as effective signs of God's grace of salvation: baptism, believers' or infant, as unrepeatable incorporation into the church; the eucharist as invoked by the Spirit, actualized memorial, sacrifice of praise and communion celebrated weekly; and the apostolic tradition, with its presbyterial and episcopal succession, the threefold ministry as a full sign of continuity and unity, and a universal priesthood of the baptized.

If Lutherans are willing to speak now of the evangelical and catholic content of the Augsburg Confession and to see themselves as a confessing communion in the church catholic, they should be open to join with other evangelical, ecumenical catholics in advancing the visible unity of a *koinonia* under the gospel. That, perhaps, is the fundamental challenge BEM puts to all of us.

Reprinted with permission, in edited form, from *Dialog* 22 (Spring, 1983): 85-93.

---

[30]Emmanuel Lanne, "The Problem of 'Reception,'" in Kinnamon, *Towards Visible Unity*, vol. 1, p. 53.

CONFERENCE PARTICIPANTS[1]

Bard, Dean W.	HPEP[2]/LCA	Chicago, IL
*Belonick, Deborah	OCA	Binghamton, NY
#Bloomquist, Karen L.	LCA	Lutheran School of Theology
*Bondi, Roberta Chesnut	UMC	Atlanta, GA
#Bowden, Raymond	PCUSA	McCormick Theological Seminary
Bowman, David J., S.J.	HPEP[2]/RCC	Chicago, IL
Bowman, Robert	CB	Elgin, IL
#Bozeman, Jean	LCA	Lutheran School of Theology
#Braaten, Carl E.	LCA	Lutheran School of Theology
*Bratt, John	CRC	Grand Rapids, MI
Brockwell, Charles	UMC	Louisville, KY
Brown, Dale W.	CB	Bethany Theological Seminary
Bruggink, Donald J.	RCA	Holland, MI
*Bull, Jennie Boyd	UFMCC	Baltimore, MD
*Burgess, Joseph A.	LCA	New York, NY
*Burke, Donald	SBC	Greenwich, CT
#Burkhart, John E.	PCUSA	McCormick Theological Seminary
Burtness, James	ALC	St. Paul, MN
Cary, W. Sterling	UCC	Oak Park, IL
*Clarkson, Shannon	UCC	Guilford, CT
Cole, Kara	FUM	Richmond, IN
#Conrad, Robert	AELC	Lutheran School of Theology
#Costigan, Richard, S.J.	RCC	Loyola University of Chicago
Cranford, Stephen	CC-D	Louisville, KY
Crow, Paul	CC-D	Indianapolis, IN
Crum, Winston F.	EpC	Evanston, IL
*Crutchfield, Kim	IEC	Decatur, GA
#Dayton, Don	ABC	Northern Baptist Theol. Seminary
Dipko, Tom	UCC	Framingham, MA
Doyle, James L.	OCA	Chicago, IL
Dreydoppel, Otto	Mor.	Victoria, MN
#Edwards, O. C.	EpC	Seabury-Western Theol. Seminary
#Egan, John	RCC	Chicago, IL
Fahey, Michael	RCC	Montreal, Ont.
Falardeau, Ernest	RCC	Albuquerque, NM
*Farmer, Kathleen A.	UMC	Dayton, OH
#Finger, Thomas	Men.	Northern Baptist Theol. Seminary
#Fischer, Robert	LCA	Lutheran School of Theology
*Ford, John	RCC	Washington, DC
Franklin, Robert	LCA	Joliet, IL
*Freeman, Arthur	Mor.	Bethlehem, PA
*Fries, Paul	RCA	New Brunswick, NJ
Fry, Franklin D.	LCA	Summit, NJ
#Fuerst, Wesley	LCA	Lutheran School of Theology
Gamble, Connolly	ABC	Valley Forge, PA
Gardner, Richard	CB	Elgin, IL
*Gatta, Julia	EpC	Storrs, CT
Hallman, Julieanne	UMC	Brockton, MA
#Harnois, Michael	LCA	Lutheran School of Theology
#Hefner, Philip	LCA	Lutheran School of Theology
*Heim, Mark	ABC	Newton, MA
*Heimer, Nancy T.	CC-D	Indianapolis, IN
#Hendel, Kurt K.	AELC	Lutheran School of Theology
*Hersch Meyer, Lauree	CB	Bethany Theological Seminary
*Hinson, E. Glenn	SB	Winston-Salem, NC
Horning, Estella	CB	Lombard, IL

144

Name	Affiliation	Location
Hotchkin, John	BCEIA³/RCC	Washington, DC
Huber, Donald L.	ALC	Pataskala, OH
*Huenemann, Ed	PCUSA	New York, NY
Huff, Bob	ALC	Janesville, WI
#Iakovos, Bishop	GO	Chicago, IL
*Jarrett, Nate	AMEZ	Chicago, IL
Jorgenson, James	OCA	Livonia, MI
Kelley, Arleon L.	UMC (guest)	New York, NY
Kilcourse, George	RCC	Louisville, KY
Kinnamon, Michael	CC-D	Indianapolis, IN
Kishkovsky, Leonid	OCA	Syosset, NY
Kleinman, Jackie	PCUSA	Columbus, OH
Kline, C. Benton	PCUSA	Decatur, GA
Kochakian, Gerabed	Armenian	Racine, WI
#Krentz, Edgar	AELC	Lutheran School of Theology
Kriese, Paul	FGC	Richmond, IN
*Lancaster, Lewis, Jr.	PCUSA	Atlanta, GA
#Laskey, Dennis	LCA	Lutheran School of Theology
#Lesher, William	LCA	Lutheran School of Theology
#Lindbeck, D.	LCA	Lutheran School of Theology
#Linnan, John E.	RCC	Catholic Theological Union
#Linss, Wilhelm	LCA	Lutheran School of Theology
#MacLennan, Ron	LCA	Lutheran School of Theology
*Madson, Meg H.	ALC	Eden Prairie, MN
*Martensen, Daniel F.	LCA	Rockville, MD
*Martyn, William	RCC	New York, NY
Matsuoka, Fumitaka	CB	Indianapolis, IN
*McElveen, William H.	Mor.	Lewisville, NC
McGinn, Bernard	RCC	Chicago, IL
*Metcalf, Patricia	PCUSA	Freeport, IL
*Moede, Gerald F.	UMC	Princeton, NJ
#Montgomery, Bp. James	EpC	Chicago, IL
Morrison, Susan M.	UMC	Randallstown, MD
#Mudge, Lewis S.	PCUSA	McCormick Theological Seminary
#Naylor, Bruce	UMC	Park Forest, IL
#Nelson, Louis J.	UCC	Glenview, IL
Norris, Edwin A., Jr.	EpC	Chicago, IL
#Osiek, Carolyn	RCC	Catholic Theological Union
#Ostdiek, Gilbert	RCC	Catholic Theological Union
#Palmquist, Dan	LCA	Lutheran School of Theology
*Parker, Thomas D.	PCUSA	McCormick Theological Seminary
*Phillips, Nancy	RCA	New York, NY
Rhodes, Dan	IEC	Decatur, GA
Richards, Clements	PCUSA	Schulenburg, TX
#Rochelle, Jay	LCA	Lutheran School of Theology
#Rooks, C. Shelby	UCC	Chicago Theological Seminary
*Russell, Letty	PCUSA	New Haven, CT
Ryan, Thomas	RCC, Canada	Montreal, Ont.
*Sakenfeld, Katharine	PCUSA	Trenton, NJ
*Sano, Roy I.	UMC	Berkeley, CA
#Scherer, James	LCA	Lutheran School of Theology
#Scholer, David	ABC	Northern Baptist Theol. Seminary
*Schreck, Christopher	RCC	Boynton Beach, FL
Selleck, Ronald	FUM	Chicago, IL
#Sherman, Franklin	LCA	Lutheran School of Theology
#Sherrer, Wayne		McCormick Theological Seminary
Smith, John W. V.	ChGod	Anderson, IN
Southard, Naomi	UMC	New York, NY

Stanwise, Ralph J.	EpC	Menomenie, WI
*Stortz, Marty	LCA	Berkeley, CA
Thomas, Margaret O.	PCUSA	New York, NY
#Tobias, Robert	LCA	Lutheran School of Theology
*Trotter, Irwin	UMC	Los Angeles, CA
*Vandervelde, George	CRC, Canada	Toronto, Ont.
*Welsh, Robert	CC-D	Indianapolis, IN
#Whitermore, David M.	Men.	Chicago, IL
Wietzke, Walter	ALC	Minneapolis, MN
Witmer, Joseph W.	BCEIA[3]/RCC	Washington, DC
#Young, Richard	EpC	Chicago, IL
#Young, William	RCC	Catholic Theological Union
*Zikmund, Barbara Brown	UCC	Berkeley, CA

---

[1]In addition to the twelve authors in this collection
[2]Hyde Park Ecumenical Project at Jesuit House
[3]Bishops' Commission for Ecumenical and Interreligious Affairs
*Members of Faith and Order Commission, National Council of Churches of Christ
#Invited guest from Chicago area